ALIEN
COVENANT

DAVID
Synthetic. Former crewmember of the *Prometheus*.

The *Covenant* – a colony ship bearing 2,000 souls in hyper-sleep ready to colonize the far-off planet Origae 6.

But a deep space shockwave, a tragic loss among the crew and an intercepted distress call leads the *Covenant* to an unidentified planet that seems even more suited to the colonists' needs.

The crew changes course for this unknown and seemingly perfect planet, but little do they know the horrors that lie in wait for them...

THE *COVENANT* CREW

JACOB BRANSON
Captain of the *Covenant*, and husband of Daniels.

DANIELS
Covenant Chief Terraformist and wife of the captain, Jaco

ORAM
Second-in-command, and Head of Life Sciences.

WALTER
The *Covenant*'s synthetic crewmember.

FARIS
Tennessee's wife and the *Covenant*'s Lander pilot.

UPWORTH
The *Covenant*'s communications expert. Ricks' wife.

PRIVATE ANKOR
Covenant security team member and assistant engineer.

KARINE
Covenant Biologist and wife of Christopher Oram.

SERGEANT LOPE
Leader of the *Covenant*'s security team. Husband of Sgt. Hallett.

RICKS
Navigator, and husband of Upworth.

PRIVATE COLE
Covenant security team member.

TENNESSEE
Covenant pilot and engineer, and husband of Faris.

SERGEANT HALLETT
Security team second-in-command, and Lope's husband.

PRIVATE LEDWARD
Covenant security team private.

PRIVATE ROSENTHAL
Covenant security team member. Involved with Private Ankor.

TITAN MAGAZINES

Editor
Neil Edwards

Senior Executive Editor
Divinia Fleary

Art Director
Oz Browne

Direct Sales and Marketing Manager
Ricky Claydon

Senior Sales Manager
Steve Tothill

Commercial Manager
Michelle Fairlamb

Brand Manager, Marketing
Lucy Ripper

Production Controller
Peter James

Production Supervisor
Maria James

Senior Production Controller
Jackie Flook

Publishing Manager
Darryl Tothill

Publishing Director
Chris Teather

Executive Director
Vivian Cheung

Publisher
Nick Landau

Distribution
US Newsstand: Total Publisher Services,
Inc. John Dziewiatkowski, 630-851-7693
US Distribution: Ingram Periodicals, Curtis
Circulation Company
UK Newsstand: Comag, 01895 444 055
UK Direct Sales Market: Diamond
Comic Distributors

Alien: Covenant Official Collector's Edition,
May 2017, published by Titan Magazines,
a division of Titan Publishing Group, 144
Southwark Street, London SE1 0UP.
TCN: 2420

Alien: Covenant TM & © 2017 Twentieth
Century Fox Film Corporation. All
Rights Reserved. Titan Authorized User.
Original Design Elements by H.R. Giger.

Thanks to Josh Izzo, Nicole Spiegel, Mary
Rafferty, Beth Goss and the rest of the
team at Twentieth Century Fox Film
Corporation, and Ridlley Scott and the cast
and crew of *Alien: Covenant.*

ISBN: 9781785861925

Printed in the US by Quad.

A CIP catalogue record for this title
is available from the British Library.

10 9 8 7 6 5 4 3 2 1

CONTENTS

The *Covenant*

Crew

Aliens

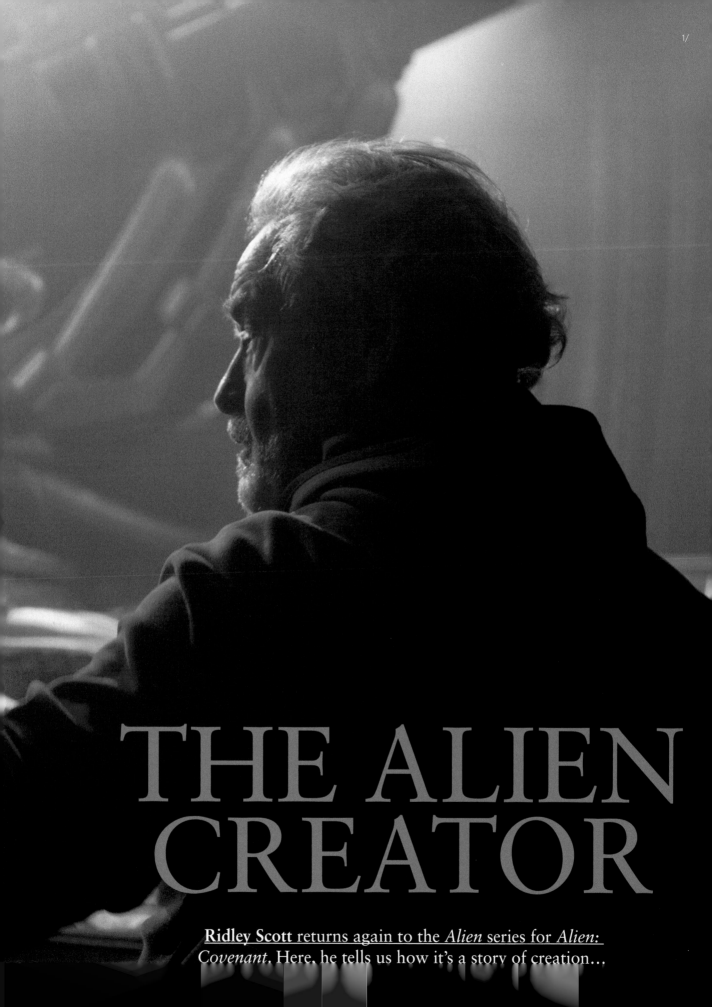

THE ALIEN CREATOR

Ridley Scott returns again to the *Alien* series for *Alien: Covenant*. Here, he tells us how it's a story of creation…

2/

Alien: Covenant Official Collector's Edition: Tell us about *Alien: Covenant* and how it fits in with the world of the original *Alien*.

Ridley Scott: The original *Alien*, as most people probably know, was fundamentally about a tin can and seven people inside it, and this thing got loose in there. So in a funny way, I always thought of *Alien* as a kind of B-movie, but really well done. Like it was A-movie quality, but the subtext was pretty basic. It's the old dark house, or seven people locked in the old dark house and who's going to die first? Who's going to survive? So they then kept that story going over the next three. And what was interesting was, no one ever asked the obvious question. "Who would make this Alien and why?" And I thought, "Well, I think I can answer who made it and why," so we began the process with *Prometheus*.

Do you think we're a biological accident? Absolutely not. First, to be sittin' here right now, talking like this, for it to be biologically convenient or a biological accident, trillions upon trillions of decisions would have had to have happened through nature to allow you to evolve to where you are right now – and me. So I think that equation is just impossible; therefore, I believe behind it all was some entity.

So that's the next thing. In *Prometheus,* they discovered the people that they called "The Engineers." Those Engineers or spacemen or aliens, in some shape or form have appeared over various forms of carving and records – Egyptian, Mayan, Aztec, cavemen – of strange beings in space, or lights in the sky. Is it all imagination or is there an element of reality attached to it? So *Prometheus* set that up.

At the end of *Prometheus,* the AI David with his head separated from his body is saved, fundamentally, by Elizabeth Shaw and they take off in an alien craft. As she said, "I don't want to go home. I want to go to where they came from, not where I came from." And that's where *Covenant* picks it up, ten years later.

And *Covenant* now gets to the point of who made the Alien and why? Don't forget, we're starting some years before *Alien*, so we're actually driving into the back entrance of *Alien*.

What is the *Covenant*?
The *Covenant* is like a pioneer ship. At some point, if we do not kill ourselves and wear out this planet, if we're here long enough, we will be able to go into deep space. I think you have to believe that. But to go into deep space, you have to also believe in the process of sleeping. Can you sleep for years? Can you deal with that kind of science? I think you have to ask the question – assume that we will. It was only 120 years ago that we hadn't flown. Now we're going beyond Mars.

So you allow that evolution to happen. I think you can assume that somebody's going to figure out how they can put you to sleep in a coma for the next ten

1 / Previous spread: Ridley Scott with the 'Space Jockey' inside the Juggernaut set 2 / Ridley Scott with Katherine Waterston (Daniels) on the Bridge set of the *Covenant* 3 / The evolution of Aliens reaches a new level with the arrival of the Neomorph

3/

years, and slow down your aging process. So there will be ships going up there that you might call pioneer ships, and the pioneers will be in hyper-sleep.

The colonists have already allotted a place [Origae 6] they think is the right distance from a light and heat source, and therefore, chances are that it will offer all the advantages of life that we had down here on Earth, because it's all down to how far you go from the sun. That's where they're going to go. So that's a covenant. They're like the settlers that came to the United States. You can think about them that way.

They'll come across the sea, they'll land, and then have to deal with the indigenous people, if there are any. But when they arrive, ironically expecting indigenous creatures, there are none. They're all dead. They see a dead planet.

Can you talk about your vision for the *Covenant* ship?

Ships are always difficult. I never, ever thought I'd do so many science fiction films. You just play around with them. You say, "I don't want to do this one I did before. What's different?" Logically, you look from the inside out. If I've got 2,000 souls on board, where's the dormitory? It's a long ship that I felt was logically like a cargo train, because it's in three sections with hexagonal junctions which are massive garages.

I thought, wherever you're going, they'll separate and each section will land as a one-time-only venture – you've landed a section which is a vast warehouse with equipment. So that's laid out on the planet.

When you do films, you think about those things, so there's a logical structure as to what you have to do.

Do the different characters in the crew of the *Covenant* have different talents in that sense?
The crew that you see are the ones

who are fundamentally flying the ship. The ones who are asleep are the real pioneers. But it's like in the Roman army: the reason why the Romans were so powerful was that every foot soldier, on his backpack, had a pickaxe. He was a man who was an expert as a mason, as well as being a soldier.

So whenever they got somewhere, the weapons would come off and they'd build a town, build a road, build a city. That's why they were so powerful. I think if you're going to do that, when you go there, you're going to build. So all those people that are asleep – except for the children, who won't know what they're going to be – but the people who are frozen and in their twenties, thirties and forties, they're probably already classified as engineers, scientists, or doctors.

What role do AIs play in the story?
I think Ash [in *Alien*] was a kind of original idea – and I always liked the idea – that every ship has an AI on board. To make it a ▶

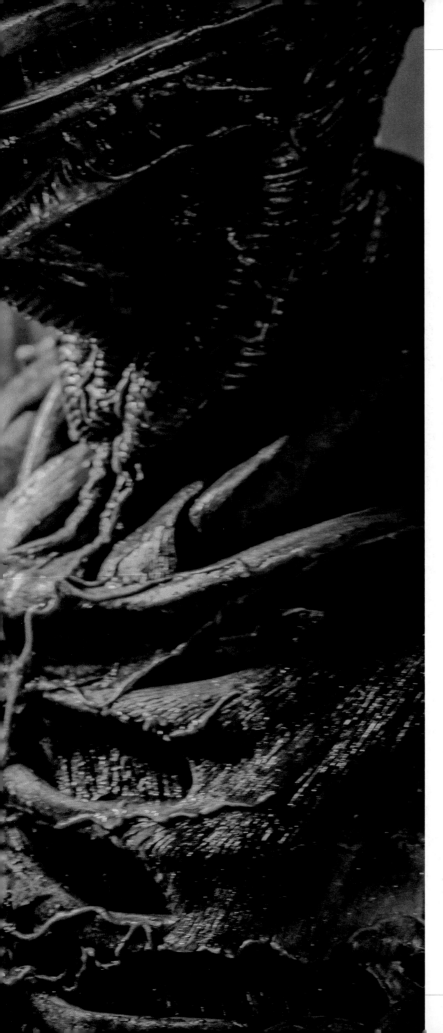

little bit more user-friendly, the AI seems to be human, so you're not talking to a robot. But nevertheless, Ash was a robot – played by Ian Holm. In this instance, the AI on board this ship is Walter. Walter is absolutely the double of David [from *Prometheus*]. So when we see Walter, we think it's David. Then we realize it's not David, it's his doppelganger now called Walter, who's another AI.

So we're in flight and he's the housekeeper and he walks around, checks things out, never has to sleep and doesn't age. When they finally land, to cut a long story short, they have a bad encounter on the planet even though the planet is kind of wondrous and spectacular and kind of threatening in its scale. At a certain point, they meet this stranger who turns up out of nowhere, and he fundamentally guides them out of a problem. They are only guessing as to where he takes them, which is a city that had been destroyed.

Once they're inside in safety, he de-hoods and we see David. David gives his past story, saying, "I've been here alone for ten years..." And to show that, he's looking at this other guy who looks completely clean-shaven and kind of normal – David's looking at him and as he leaves that scene, he says, "Welcome, brother." So now they've connected, and David is clearly not a good guy.

Tell us about working with Michael Fassbender.
When I did *Prometheus*, I always had my eye on Michael. We came up with the idea then of his fascination with *Lawrence of Arabia*, so there's that subtext and we dyed his hair blond and he actually looked a little bit like Peter O'Toole did in *Lawrence*, and then Michael would mimic Peter O'Toole.

Michael is a great actor, but at the same time, he's got a great sense of humor. I always want to have humor in everything I do. So there's quite a lot of wit in this ▸

4 / The Xenomorph is set to return in two more sequels, Scott has revealed

▶ film, certainly between the two AIs. There are challenges, but I think the challenges are kind of interesting. They're truisms. They're logical questions you might ask of something or someone that's been created.

There's a great scene where it becomes about how you can do everything mathematically, scientifically. You can memorize the telephone directory, but what you can't do is be creative. So David says, "That's nonsense. I'll show you – play music."

So the scene where he plays the flute, which I think is pretty good, he shows Walter how he can be creative – the subtext being that the human race is over. Whether it's going to take another hundred years or whatever, what's going to take our place is probably David, who thinks he's kingpin. So it's kind of about taking over the world.

It's a metaphor for *Big Brother*, really – we are relying more and more on technology and less and less on our ingenuity and hands. Even though technology is ingenuity, if we don't watch it, we're going to have large brains and puny bodies, because we won't be actually physically doing anything… I think that's where they think it's going to go.

How about Katherine Waterston?
She did a film with Joaquin Phoenix [*Inherent Vice*]. It was directed by Paul Thomas Anderson – I like his work a lot. I watched it and as well as Joaquin, who is always spectacularly good, I watched this girl, and thought, "Who the hell is that?"

From that we cast her, because I needed somebody who was physically imposing, tall, athletic and hopefully a good actress. And she's special. I think what's interesting is, both she and Billy Crudup come from the theater. I'm sure I've dealt with people before from the theater, but they weren't theatrical in that sense.

They very much brought to bear their technique – their knowledge and sensitivity, theatrically.

When you're doing a film like this, which has people dying and is constantly stressful and it has to be a constant show of fear, there are many colors of fear and remorse. In a person who's had a theater background, they dig deep and can pull that out, so they helped enormously in that respect and I really enjoyed working with both of them.

Can you tell us about Billy Crudup's character, Oram?
He's always in the shadow of Daniels' husband, because Daniels' husband was beloved – a scientist, an engineer, a jack-of-all-trades and a genius at everything.

He was a hard man to follow, so when he died, it was like really, truly losing the leader.

Oram was always passed over as not quite being up to scratch, but nevertheless very good at what he did – a very good pilot, very good at varying things – but people go through these psychological examinations and every astronaut is examined very carefully, psychologically. If you're going to go up there with four astronauts and spend a year with them, you'd better get along, or you'd better have a psychology that enables you to see past problems and deal with them rather than having a tantrum every three seconds.

So in that sense, he was a good second-in-command, but a bit like a vice president, who is suddenly

5 / Director Ridley Scott directs his cast as the *Covenant* crew on set, including Michael Fassbender (left) as Walter

5 /

pristine. **Do you think about those things in terms of the design?**
This is not a grungy ship – this is a pioneer ship, on a scientific mission. So by the time you get to the first *Alien*, you're maybe 100 years on from this, where they've now quite clearly become capable of actually digging and mining off the surface of planets.

What were some of the biggest challenges you faced during the making of the film?
Making it scary... designing the aliens – because I've been there before. The chest-burster in the original *Alien*, that wasn't H.R. Giger. He didn't design that. What happened was he had done this dinosaur-looking thing and I said, "Listen, you've got enough to do." So I drew something on an envelope, and a guy called Roger Dicken, who has a little workshop in Windsor, created the chest-burster. It was very successful. I think it was hard to beat that, so that was one of the biggest challenges – how do I make it better than that? I felt it had to be more of a creature with arms and legs.

It's coming out of Ledward's back this time, which means it'll be rather big, but you don't want it that small as he's growing fast. We have no idea of certain biology and how fast growth can be. Plant life in a desert lies dormant for years without one rainstorm, and literally hours later, there are flowers. That's fast growth. If you sat and watched or stop-motioned that, you'd see it happen.

There are some big scares in this movie. How would you describe the tone of *Alien: Covenant*?
I hope it's really scary. I hope it makes you uneasy and I hope your heart starts pounding. I hope you have a very dry throat, but you've got to watch the screen. I hope it doesn't give you any nightmares, but then again it might give you a few nightmares. That's a good thing... ●

vulnerable when the other guy is no longer there. He's right in the spotlight and because he's not really ready for it, he's very nervous and fragile, but he has a strong, advisory wife, Karine. When I first said the crew had to be couples, I thought it made sense so they can literally be a husband and wife, and also functionaries. That's how it would need to be, because you're going away forever.

All the *Alien* movies are known for their rich sound design. Can you talk about how you bring the world of the creatures to life audibly?
Sound is so important in film language. Sometimes film-makers don't include music at all and that's a statement in itself. So silence is also music. For example, suddenly everything goes silent and you think, "Oh my God, something nasty's going to happen," or it gets very noisy. That's a choice you have to make. But I think one thing was for sure: I wanted to not forget Jerry Goldsmith, who did a spectacularly good score for *Alien*.

The composer, Jed Kurzel, appreciates that and was not afraid to include some of Jerry's score. For example, when they start talking about the planet and say, "It looks really old," we literally just used Jerry Goldsmith's score. It's so archetypal and well-known that people love it. It's hard to better it.

The first *Alien* had that sort of grungy feel. This film is very

CONCEPT ART - THE *COVENANT*
The *Covenant* – a colony vessel
carrying 2,000 colonists in hyper-
sleep to Origae 6, before a distress
signal from an unknown planet puts
the entire mission in jeopardy...

MICHAEL FASSBENDER AS

DAVID/ WALTER

Michael Fassbender on playing David and Walter – two similar-looking but very different synthetic models…

Alien Covenant Official Collector's Edition: Why do you think the Alien films still scare people so much after all this time? Michael Fassbender: I suppose it's the concept of space and what's out there – that it's very hard to believe that we're the only species that exists in the universe. And then I think of the idea of parasites – things that would use us as a host – as quite a disturbing concept. For me personally, I always remember from the first Alien film, John Hurt and the Xenomorph bursting out of his stomach, and that's always stayed with me. I suppose it's that idea of something growing inside us, using our bodies to basically grow a seed into something living. Parasites living within us is quite a freaky idea.

What do you think makes the Aliens of the Alien films so unique?
I think they're a beautiful design. There's an insect-like quality to them, but they're very much stand-alone creatures, and I think they're quite beautiful. The head of the alien is a very aerodynamic, smooth design, and it's quite a beautiful thing. As much as it is horrific, there's a beauty to it.

> "
> # I think hopefully the audience will be wary of Walter…
> "

What are your fondest memories from watching the Alien films?
Again, it would be the first Alien. I got an opportunity to watch it when I was quite young, maybe 11 or 12. Usually my parents wouldn't let me see films that were R-rated or even over-15, due to the violent content of such films. But if they felt like there was something that had a sophistication or intelligence to it, they would allow me to watch it. I suppose what's great about that first film is it's very believable. You disappear into that world and very quickly you can relate to it, even though you're dealing with something that's in the future.

I think it's also the way that Ridley Scott mixes things like a microwave on board the ship with holograms and systems that are way ahead of our time and what we can imagine people would be using in the future. It's something that we can relate to and therefore invest more in. Ridley did the same with Blade Runner, with the idea that Deckard is eating noodles, and that sort of Asian-type food would be the food of the future because it feeds so many people in Asia and it's so sustainable. So those details of things that are old-fashioned or traditional, mixed with something that's futuristic have a very powerful effect. ▶

▶ **How does it feel to return to this franchise with Ridley Scott?**
It's great. I think all of the actors – I feel I can speak for all of the actors – feel very privileged and it's kind of like being a kid again, wandering around on the sets. I've done a few films on this scale, but never have I been on a film where the sets have been so impressive, so complete. If I'm on the ship set, the *Covenant*, I feel like I'm on the spaceship. All these production designs are so detailed and so sophisticated.

I didn't expect to be as surprised again, coming on to this set, but I have been. Each time when I walk onto a new set, it's a treat. It's a rare thing, as well, with films that are this high-concept. There's a lot of green screen, usually. We have been using some of that in this, but a lot of it is there for you to explore and to touch and interact with, and that's a real rarity these days.

What are the differences between the two characters you play, David and Walter?
I think the David Eight model was designed to allow the synthetic to develop human-like qualities and characteristics, and we very much see that in David. David has characteristics like pride and vanity, which are very human traits, and that ended up disturbing people. They weren't very comfortable with it, so they decided to design the later models with fewer of those programming functions.

Walter is just very much a functioning synthetic that operates through logic and without any human emotional thread. He doesn't incorporate concepts like vanity or jealousy or gratitude. He doesn't fall in love with characters, whereas we saw a strange relationship between Shaw

2 /

1 / Previous page: Walter monitors his human crewmates aboard the *Covenant*

2 / Inside David's sinister laboratory

3 / Keeping a watchful eye over the sleeping colonists…

4 / David and his mirror image in the White Room, reflecting the fact his model's appearance has been replicated in the Walter model

and David. There is a bond that develops which is a very human one, and human flaws that come with it. But Walter is purely there to look after the crew and the *Covenant* – he's like a super-butler.

What were the challenges of playing two characters?
Different haircuts! I mean, really it's kind of down to that. I think Robert Mitchum said he had two types of acting – on a horse and off it. [*Laughs*] So I guess I just kind of stuck to those parameters, really. You can have a lot of fun with the David character, because he's received no maintenance or servicing for the last ten years. So the idea is that these human traits have started to overcome the synthetic ones – and I've treated him like a serial killer really. He's afraid of things leaving him, so he incubates them. Like a Jeffrey

Dahmer-type character, David doesn't want things he loves to leave him, so he kills them and keeps them in caskets or preserved one way or the other.

When we last saw David, he was a severed head and body. Where do we start with him here?
We did shoot a prologue to the film with Shaw, and we pick up where we left Shaw and David. They're in one of the Engineers' ships, trying to find the origin of the Engineers, and their home planet. We could sense that the time that's passed has caused things to become a little bit fractious between the two of them. You get the impression that Shaw is wary of David, and I think he just wears on her nerves. He's like this lovesick stalker in space, which is an interesting concept. But Shaw does have sympathy ▶

3 /

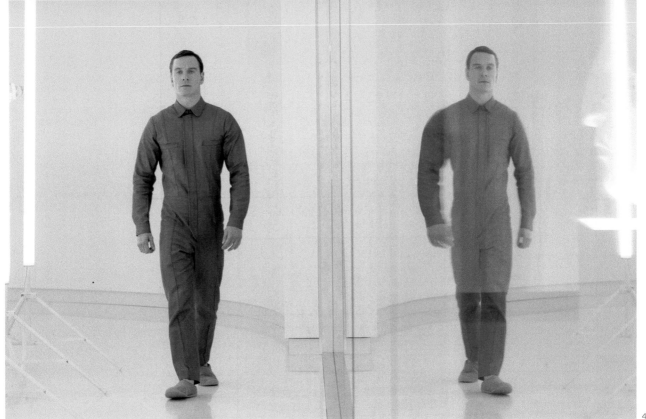

4 /

for him, and she does put him back together.

Once David's put back together, we quickly realize he's a danger to her and to the Engineers, and that he's become obsessed with the idea of creation. Peter Weyland was David's creator, and Weyland was then obsessed with the idea of finding his own creator. That's struck a chord with David, and I think he sees himself as a creator. He wants to give birth to something, and he starts to explore that desire.

Should we be wary of David's fellow synthetic, Walter?
I think hopefully the audience will be wary of Walter, just because it's fun, but they needn't be, because he's very straightforward. He is first and foremost there to protect and to serve, like good police officers should do. When I studied the character, I was trying to work out how to distinguish between Walter and David. I always thought Mr. Spock was a good reference for this character – he's purely logical and devoid of emotion, even if those around him, particularly Daniels, search for some sort of emotional connectivity with him; that's not really there.

We play with that a little bit and there is a bit of ambiguity there, to keep the suspense levels up and to keep the audience engaged in that possibility – is he protecting her, or is it going to turn nasty? Is he becoming obsessive about her, as David did with Shaw? And is David going to have an influence on Walter that's going to determine the fate of the crew?

Can you set the stage for what goes on in the *Covenant* in the beginning and why it is that they decide to reroute?
They hit a stellar spontaneous ignition – it's basically a space storm, let's say. When that occurs, they have their recharging sails out, so the *Covenant* experiences some damage.

It's a ship that has something like 2,000 colonists on it who are going to start life anew on a new planet – Origae 6 – and they're on their way there when they hit this storm. Walter is concerned that the colonists might get damaged, so he wakes the command crew out of hyper-sleep – and soon after they've woken up, they hear a beacon. They hear what seems to be a distress call, which happens to be Shaw's signal from a planet which seems to fulfill all the necessary requirements for them to start life – air that's breathable and fresh water, foliage and sustainability – a sustainable planet. So they decide – rather than going back into cryo-sleep, which will mean another six years before they arrive at their destination – to take a look at this planet. They shouldn't have done that.

The planet is a lot like Earth, but it's sinister and there's something foreboding about it when the *Covenant* crew arrives.
I suppose what's foreboding about it is David. It used to be the Engineers' home planet, and it was populated by them. David released the pathogen, which was ironic, because the Engineers designed the pathogen as a weapon and David uses the weapon against them and wipes them out. But they have a shield surrounding the planet, which can prevent people from entering or leaving it. So once the *Covenant* sends down a scouting group onto the planet, they're left stranded there, and their landing ship gets destroyed. A few things happen in terms of some of these organisms that are living on the planet. One of the parasites, which develop into Neomorphs – manages to get into the character Hallett. So the first Neomorph is born, and starts to wreak havoc.

What can you tell us about these Neomorphs?
I don't know a great deal about them. They're big, they're fast,

5 /

they're very angry. It's not my speciality. I just breed them. [*Laughs*]

Tell us about David's state of mind when the crew meet him. You touched on the fact that he's not had maintenance for ten years.
David, when we catch up with him, is kind of like a surfer dude – his hair's grown long, and he has let himself go a little bit. That was something we were toying with – the concept that he was dying his hair. He had become obsessed with the *Lawrence Of Arabia* character, Peter O'Toole's character in the film, and dyed his hair blond. Over the years, obviously, he's run out of dye and his roots have grown out and he's kind of scraggly. He's been living alone on this planet, doing his little experiments and obviously ▶

5 / Walter is a loyal friend to Daniels (Katherine Waterston)

6 / David's appearance has changed after 10 years on the planet

7 / Synthetic Walter takes the lead as the *Covenant* landing party explores the planet

8 / Even a synthetic can bear battle scars

something has happened to Shaw. He killed her, essentially, to prevent her from leaving him, and he's been experimenting with other life forms on the planet. David's exploring the creative side of himself. He's been playing music, he's been painting, and he's somewhat of a Doctor Moreau-type figure. So the crew comes across him, and he saves their lives.

David's a very adaptable and opportunistic character. He has a plan, but the plan is always fluid. Once he becomes aware that there are colonists on this ship, he becomes very interested in that, because as a scientist he's now got lots of subjects to play with. Essentially the *Covenant*'s going to be his ticket off this planet, so he's pretty sinister.

When Walter and David meet, what do they make of each other?
I think the crew – in particular Daniels – are very wary of David. They're all aware that he's a synthetic, as he looks exactly like Walter. We associate it with cars – there are different models, and they're recognizable to humans. So everyone's aware that he's a synthetic from the get-go. Walter decides to go and investigate, and in doing so, realizes there's an emotional side to David, which he finds quite disturbing and he draws it to our attention that David's a synthetic who has been without servicing for ten years and exactly what that does to an AI. David tries to educate Walter. I think he sees himself as an older brother, and flirts with the idea of the two of them going into cahoots. But Walter's programming just doesn't allow for that, and eventually David realizes he's getting in the way of his master plan.

You've said Daniels is wary of David. What about David towards Daniels? Is it an attraction similar to his attraction toward Shaw?
David, I think, finds these strong female characters attractive, and

he's really an old romantic. So he's a little bit confused. He does have a scene with Daniels where he tries to simulate sex. He's got a strange sexuality. He's in a very confused state, because he feels these human characteristics – jealousy, vanity, pride – but he also has these sexual desires, which he obviously can't act out, but wants to.

How do you think audiences will see *Alien: Covenant* in relation to

9 / Walter helps ready the repairs to the *Covenant*'s solar sails

10 / Examining a specimen on board the *Covenant*

the other *Alien* movies?
This film, for me, is in a lot of ways like the first *Alien*, in terms of the way Ridley's shooting it. It's very gritty and dark, and Dariusz [Wolski] lights it that way. And yet it's still got the big concept and set-pieces. He's brought the two worlds together. But from the get-go, when the *Covenant* hits that space storm, it sets a series of things in motion which doesn't

industry and an acknowledgement of talent in all departments.

Ridley will pick actors on the fringes of popularity, from films that are more arthouse, and there's great diversity in his cast. Also it's the way that he notices somebody in a department and how valuable they are and how good they are at their job. He's an all-rounder, and that would be selling him short because he's a master filmmaker and there are not many out there. They're a very rare breed.

How has Ridley helped you differentiate your two characters?
We try different things out, and both of us like to try and find the humor in everything. That's something that I really enjoy about playing David – trying to find the funny beats with him, even though he's grotesque and a lot of the things that are happening are grotesque. To try and get the audience to laugh even for a beat, always helps open an audience up. All of us let our guards down when we laugh, so we're more likely to experience other things like shock and horror to a fuller effect when we're not so guarded or we haven't been numbed because there's been a lack of humor in there.

Ridley's very mischievous and creative – his notes can come totally out of leftfield, but also be very provocative and simple. He doesn't say a great deal, which is great. He gives very short, concise notes, and always in a way that will allow you to go and cultivate that note, as opposed to giving you a direct order.

Your characters have a few fight scenes, especially when you're fighting yourself. How was that?
Working with myself? It's the most pleasurable experience of my career, I have to say. [*Laughs*] No, it was a nightmare, really. The fight stuff was a bit tricky. Just learning both sides of the fight was a little bit of a head-wrecker, but we got there in the end. •

stop until the end of the film. So ten minutes into the film, things start to heat up and it becomes pretty relentless, especially once they hit the planet and Hallett gets infected. I think this is going to be the scariest one out of all the films. But I would say that. [*Laughs*]

Ridley is seen as a real actor's director. What is it like working with him?
It's a one-off experience working

with Ridley. Of the actors that have worked with him that I've talked to, everyone's very aware that there's no one like Ridley, certainly that I've come across or read about or heard other people in the industry talk about.

He's very special, and he comes from an art background so he's very aware of a frame, and very knowledgeable about what should be in it. He's seen everything and has a passion for talent in the

THE
NEOMORPH

Alien: Covenant sees the birth of a whole
new alien – the Neomorph. **Ridley Scott**
and visual effects supervisor **Charley Henley**
tell us about this terrifying creation…

When the *Covenant* crew land on the Engineers' planet, they soon literally stumble across a new lifeform that has been mutated by the black accelerant from the local ecosystem.

When disturbed, the egg sac pods release a spore that enters a host's body via their facial openings, such as the nose or ear. An agonizing death awaits as the spore gestates and grows inside its host, before bursting from them. The Neomorph's dorsal spikes and pointed head rip through the host's back as it emerges, or alternatively it is born through the mouth, ripping the host's jaw apart as it comes out.

What emerges is a horrifying and rapidly growing alien that is hostile from birth. Bipedal and tailed, the Neomorph is distinguished by its almost translucent appearance and its deadly fang-like teeth. You cannot run or hide from the Neomorph…

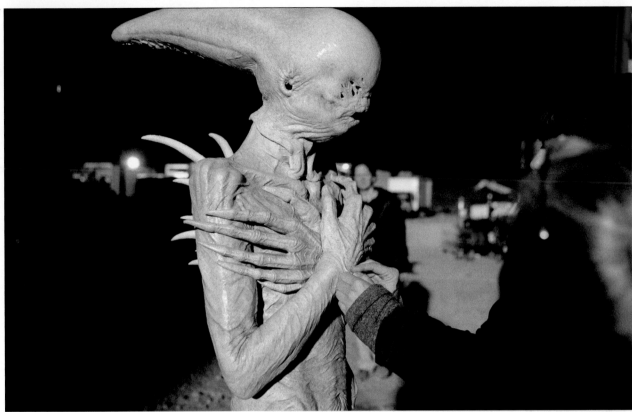

3 /

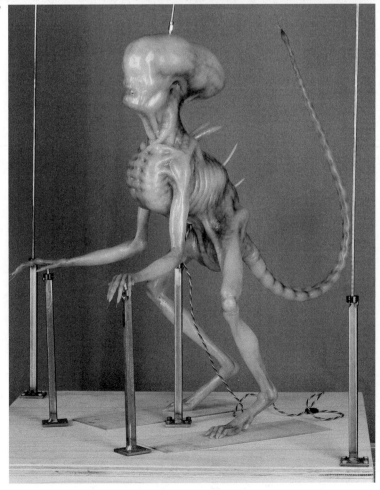

CREATING
THE NEOMORPH

CHARLEY HENLEY, VISUAL EFFECTS
SUPERVISOR, ON CREATING
THE NEOMORPH:

The creature work on *Alien: Covenant* is
obviously a major part of this particular film.
We're introducing some new ones, which are
exciting for me, because it's a new
development. One in particular – the Neomorph
– is a favorite, and the design process of
creating him is interesting. Ridley brought a lot
of references to the table and illustrations of
how he wanted this creature to be. We had a
good guide there, but working out exactly how
the Neomorph moves and animates has been an
interesting challenge, and Conor O'Sullivan and
the Creatures department have been pivotal in
designing the creature and building maquettes
of his full form. One of the interesting parts of
him is his jaw action. Ridley found references of
a shark called the goblin shark, where literally its
whole jaw can dislocate and fire forward to grab
its prey and pull it back in. It had a lovely quality
to it, besides the nasty mechanics of its mouth.

We're rolling in references like that, as well
as looking at a lot of real animal motion to find
a balance, so that he feels like he moves in a
realistic way but is still a somewhat freaky
creature, and pretty scary. I'm looking forward to
seeing the final product of the Neomorph.

1 / Previous spread
The Neomorph design
by Creatures Supervisor
Conor O'Sulllivan and
his team

2 / A stunt performer
is suited up as the
Neomorph

3 / The newborn
Neomorph is brought
to life using puppetry...

4 / Creature design
showing that the
Neomorph is bipedal
in its movements

5 / A creature design
showing the Neomorph
ready to attack

BIRTHING THE ALIEN...

CHARLEY HENLEY ON A NEOMORPH BIRTH:

The Neomorph bursts out of Hallett. That's a particular example, where Conor O'Sullivan created a dummy version of Hallett which he can launch the creature physically through with lots of blood effects, gore and a placenta bag. Inside the placenta bag is the creature that bursts out, and because of the crazy action and the fact that it's full of gore and nasty bits, it works really well on camera, and Hallett's dummy looks amazing!

We'll do things to enhance the dummy, like put the real actor's eyes on it [using CGI], and in the case of Hallett's birth, the creature bursts out of his mouth. Then it comes out of the egg sac and slides off him, so we're adding in some animation. The material looks fantastic with the real blood and the real model that's been built, so we just do a little enhancement to that.

Once it's fallen out, to have the creature get up and start crawling away and run into the grass is something that there are limitations to doing in puppeteering. Effectively we can get more out of doing it in visual effects now, because we can get muscle movement and freedom to move him in a way that we couldn't do practically.

6 /

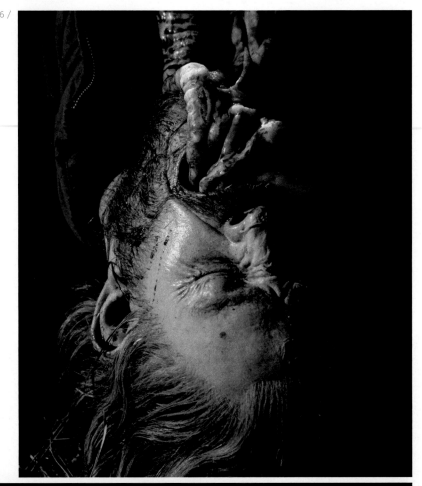

7 /

6 / Hallett suffers agonizing pain as the Neomorph begins to emerge

7 / The newborn Neomorph is almost translucent in color

8 / The Neomorph in its egg sac is born...

9 /

10 /

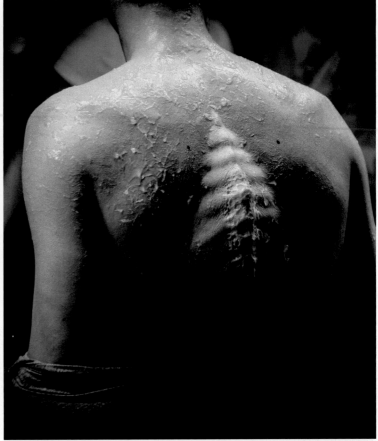

11 /

BACK-BURSTER

RIDLEY SCOTT ON FILMING THE 'BACK-BURSTER' SCENE:

Benjamin Rigby [who plays Ledward] was literally a fantastic twitcher. I said, "Are you all right? You're going to hurt your back. Take it easy." But he said, "No, I'm fine." He was swinging over backwards, so it seemed like he was going to hurt his back, but he didn't.

I loved the idea of sticking Ledward in Medbay, because then he's going to get all the gear off him, they're going to strip him down and there we see the beginning of something on his back which then has a little evolution of spurting a little aerosol of blood and infection.

As Faris backs off, she already thinks she's infected, and she races to the Bridge. When she comes back you see the thing is strong enough to push through and separate the spine from the individual roots. It's pushing, and it bites its way out.

9 / The baby Neomorph is manipulated by means of rods

10 / Ledward (Benjamin Rigby), is impregnated

11 / A special effects technician does his grisly work...

12 / Ledward is in agony as the Neomorph starts to emerge!

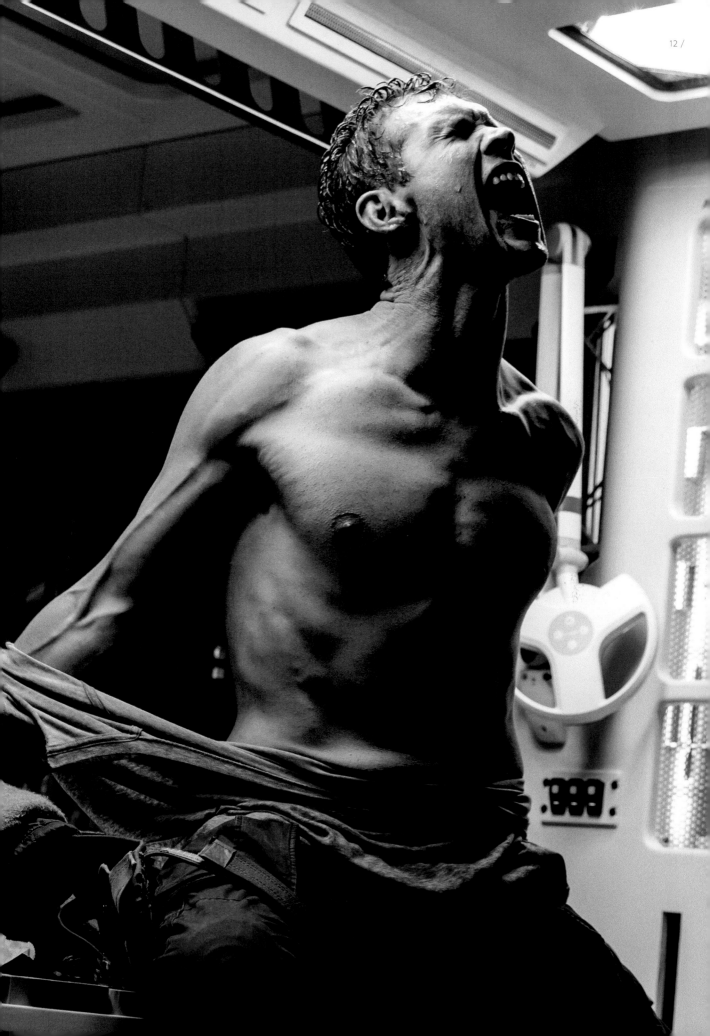

KATHERINE WATERSTON AS DANIELS

Katherine Waterson on playing Daniels, the *Covenant*'s Chief Terraformist, who deals with personal loss before discovering her heroic side when confronting the horrors unleashed upon her crew…

Alien: Covenant Official Collector's Edition: What is it like to be part of the *Alien* franchise?
Katherine Waterston: It's amazing to be a part of it. It's such a beloved entity already and it's just lovely to enter into something you feel that people already have such a strong connection with.

Ridley has a long history of strong female characters in his films. How does it feel to be taking on that mantle here?
I feel like Ridley has always shown women as they are, as I see them in the world, really in a complete and honest way. Ridley's one of those directors who's always portrayed women in a believable way, or he's been attracted to those kinds of characters.

What's your character, Daniels', role in the crew?
Daniels is third-in-command at the beginning of the film, and she's Chief Terraformist on the *Covenant* ship – she's basically like a space gardener, so when they arrive on Origae 6, she'll be responsible for setting up the environment and growing things so that they have food to eat.

> " I don't think Daniels fancies herself as any kind of heroic figure… "

Set the scene for us. What happens to the *Covenant*?
At the beginning of the film, the crew is forced awake from hyper-sleep. Normally they are brought out of hyper-sleep in a very slow way, as it's very physically taxing to wake up out of it that quickly. Of course people have probably seen the original *Alien*, in which that also happened.
There's been a malfunction on the ship and when their pods open and they all start to climb out, they realize that their captain's module isn't opening and he's killed in there in front of us all; in front of Daniels, his wife. That's the first time we see Daniels in the film, and of course that loss is something that she carries with her throughout the story.

Daniels and the AI Walter have a special bond. How do you think that came about?
I imagine that before the events of the film, she just liked him. He's very different from [the AI] David. Walter's just delightful, and very kind. But then I think she comes to really rely on him after Jacob dies and I also think she feels more comfortable around him than the rest of the crew, because he is emotionally limited.
It may be easier for her to be around someone who doesn't really understand what she's going through, so she can be left alone with her grief a little bit. When you lose someone, you often also have to be aware of the emotions of the other people around ▶

you, and she doesn't have to do that with him. She feels that he is protective of her, but she also doesn't really have to engage with him, so there's a kind of ease there. I think she feels close to him, or has a connection to him, because they are the only two single, sentient beings on the ship. Everybody else is partnered up. So from the moment that she loses Jacob, she immediately becomes an outsider on the ship in a way.

What's it like to act against someone who's playing an AI?
It is fascinating to play scenes with someone who's playing a synthetic. I feel a little bit like I'm getting to time travel to maybe three generations ahead of my own. Maybe it's less, maybe it's more. But it is coming, and [sentient] AIs are being developed now.

It's chilling and bizarre and

funny and weird and obviously that's such a testament to Michael Fassbender's work as an actor that I'm so convinced by what he's doing. It's truly surreal.

How do you see Daniels' alliance with Tennessee?
There are two people in the crew that Jacob and I are closest to, and that's Tennessee and his wife, Faris. As the film progresses, Tennessee and I are thrown into a lot of circumstances together, and are further bonded by the horrors and losses that we both experience in the film. Danny [McBride] is just amazing – he's such a joy to work with and so lovely, and I think, really moving in the film.

How would you describe the Neomorphs?
Fast. It's just so scary. We have this incredible stunt crew on this

film and Ridley puts them into the scenes as much as possible. It's not all done against a green screen. We can really feel what it's like to be attacked by these creatures.

Those guys were so incredible at mimicking the movements of what they will put onto the film later. It makes our job so much more fun because it feels so real.

When David saves them, how does Daniels feel about him?
I think that Daniels is very sharp. She's the kind of person who is clear-headed in a crisis, and there are a few things that David says initially that don't sound quite right to her.

Then, when even Walter doesn't quite know what to make of David, I think she's more concerned, but there is no other option. So she has to follow him and trust him, because they're all

1 / Previous spread: Katherine Waterston as Daniels

2 / Daniels wears her late husband Jacob's clothes as she talks to her friend, the AI Walter (Michael Fassbender)

3 / Daniels on board the *Covenant*

4 / Daniels feels a sense of foreboding when the crew land on the mysterious planet

5 / Daniels prepares for hyper-sleep in the *Covenant's* Nursery

3 /

4 /

5/

► in danger and he knows something about this place.

When you do finally come up against David in a fight, what was that like?
It's so much fun! It's like being on the playground. Michael is so sinister in the scene where he attacks me, and again, it's sort of the same as being chased by the stunt guys, and the wonderful costumes they put them in. It drops you into the reality of the situation really easily and makes my job a lot easier. It's really fun to learn fight choreography and explore that aggressive side of myself that I am not often invited to explore in my personal life or on film.

Daniels seems like an unwilling hero. How do you feel about her journey?
I think people often wonder how they will handle terrifying or challenging situations. You don't really know what you're made of until you're confronted with a crisis, so at the beginning of the film, Daniels is capable, she's smart and she's good at her job, but I don't think she fancies herself as any kind of heroic or particularly tough figure.

But it just so happens, as the events of the film unfold, she's able to function well and think clearly in moments of crisis. That was easier for me to relate to or understand than this idea that she was born cool and tough and ready for battle. I don't know anybody like that.

How does *Alien: Covenant* compare with the other *Alien* films?
I think like the original *Alien*, there's a relentless feeling to the chaos and the anxiety in this film; once it gets going, it doesn't really stop until the end. I think Ridley wanted to make another scary picture. He wanted it to be gory, and it is. I think it's going to freak people out.

What makes the *Alien* films so terrifying?
The *Alien* films are so terrifying because the characters are so believable. They're regular people, like any of us, who find themselves in a situation they are really ill-equipped to handle. You're stuck somewhere and you can't get away and something's coming for you. I think that when he was making the first *Alien*, Ridley understood fear and portrayed it really truthfully, and I think he's doing that again now. ●

6 / Daniels arms herself for a terrifying confrontation

BILLY CRUDUP AS
ORAM

Billy Crudup tells us about playing
Oram, the *Covenant*'s accidental leader
and man of faith...

Alien: Covenant Official
Collector's Edition:
Who is Oram and
how does he fit into
the *Covenant* crew?
Billy Crudup: He's the first mate,
which means he's second-in-
command, and he's also in charge
of the Life Sciences division.

Everybody who has
volunteered to be a part of this
expedition has some sort of
philosophical agenda. It's a one-
way trip, and you're going to
essentially start a new tribe
of humanity in a different part
of the galaxy. For Oram, there's
a theological perspective to his
motivation to being a part of this
mission; his belief system seems to
be a guiding force in most of the
things that drive him.

Each of the crewmembers come
at this journey from a different
perspective, a different motivation.
They have a belief that, like all
pioneers, there's something else
out there for them to find. For
Oram, it's really a celebration of
his own humanity; the potential to
be able to colonize another planet.
That's paying tribute to God, as
he believes it. He wants to spread
that message and that belief
system throughout the known

world, or worlds, or galaxy. This is
an opportunity for him to literally
explore the depths of God's
creation, and figuratively as well.

> "
> There's a
> genuine
> psychological
> break that
> happens in
> Oram.
> "

**When the shockwave happens,
what is Oram's role in events?**
Their hyper-sleep is interrupted, as
seems to be typical for the *Alien*
movies, and there has been some
damage to the ship, and to one
crewmember in particular – the
captain. He becomes incapacitated
inside his pod and perishes. That
leaves Oram as the captain.

There's a reason Oram was
second-in-command and not
first-in-command – he's really not
as capable a leader as he thinks
he is. When he's thrown into this
position, he has to manage that

anxiety and fear whilst handling a
crew that is dubious of his potential
to lead and probably a little bit
dubious of his religious beliefs.
[They're] concerned that maybe
he thinks it is an act of providence
that he was chosen, so he might not
make the most rational and sound
judgments in the end.

**Does he feel pressure on him to
get the colony situated?**
There's no question about it.
The weight of these 2,000-plus
souls, for him, is enormous
and overwhelming. There's a
tremendous amount of self-doubt
at his capacity to manage his
own fear about leading this many
people into the unknown. That's
a big part of the story in terms
of what we're playing; how he
relates to the other crewmembers
and how he, ultimately, finds some
sense of confidence and clarity
and moral authority in trying to
defend them.

**How do Oram's religious beliefs
affect his relationship with the rest
of the crew?**
He alienates himself from people
because unconsciously for him,
he's dogmatic in his belief system
and judgmental about how ▶

▶ people go about living their lives. It's a way of being asleep – of sleepwalking through life. To not believe in something, to not believe in a purpose, as given to you by a creator in the form of life, for Oram is a kind of absurd way to get through the day. So he's not well socialized and that scares people. His wife, Karine, on the other hand, sees his insecurities, and sees that this is not dogma in him.

What happens when Oram hears the strange signal from the planet?
When he hears this voice, he connects it to his faith, insofar as everything happens for a reason. So if the ship broke down here, and there is the recovery of a transmission of a lone human voice, in his mind it must be because he was given the opportunity to save this soul. He begins to act with that viewpoint in mind and that's intimidating to some of the crewmembers. Though he wears it close to his chest, it's still on their mind.

Why does Oram change the ship's course?
There are several things at play. One, the ship is compromised at that moment. There's tremendous trauma for the crew, being awoken from hyper-sleep to find their captain being incinerated.

There's the recognition that there exists a planet that had not yet been mapped, that has many of the same characteristics of the planet we'd previously vetted. In addition to that, with the notion that there's a distress signal coming from the planet, there's a mandate that you have to look into it.

For Oram, he has justifiable reasons to approach the planet. It doesn't mean they're going to necessarily colonize it, but at least they're going to get a lay of the land and see if there's somebody in need. It all feels very rational to him. It seems like a sound argument to make and one, also, that the crew – with the exception of Daniels – are very supportive of, because they don't want to

2 /

get back in the hyper-sleep pods. Oram is feeling pretty stoked about himself at that moment.

Tell us about the Engineers' Dreadnought that the crew comes across. It must be very unsettling for the crew to find vestiges of a lost alien civilization.
We're talking at a point in the future where humans have not yet discovered alien civilizations. They probably have a growing awareness that that's a high likelihood, and while there's a probability that it's an alien civilization, there's also a possibility that it's a human civilization that had been colonized some way or another. [The statues and remains are] certainly humanoid figures, and there are vestiges of some kind of comprehensible system, so more than anything, it's the awe of the scale of what's been built or has found its way here [that's unsettling].

Again, because we have a human voice that has been transmitting to us, most of us are certain there's a human element to this enterprise. It would be

tantamount to coming upon the Valley of the Kings for the first time. You have these enormous man/dog figures and you don't say, "Wow, giant man/dogs were real." You say, "Wow, these are icons that people built – that they worshipped." That's what's going through Oram's mind – maybe it was an abandoned outpost for some sort of religious or research colony.

Take us to the moment when things start to go horribly wrong for the mission.
There is a very quick turn for the worse where, seemingly out of nowhere, with no visual reference, two of the crewmembers become violently ill and one of them is with my wife, who is away from me. All we have to communicate with are these earpieces, and to hear the terror and the panic that's beginning to set in through that device is traumatic. Because he's the one in charge, Oram's attempting to balance experiencing the trauma, saving his wife and maintaining leadership of this crew, and that's more than he can

1 / Previous spread
Oram discovers the Egg Room and its disturbing contents

2 / Oram's faith causes friction between him and his crew

3 / Oram is at first elated to discover a new world to explore where he can spread his beliefs

4 / As the Aliens attack, Oram realizes the dire situation he has put his crew in

handle. So he just loses it for a little while.

And then David comes along... From the moment that they get back to the Lander and alien beings appear, it becomes a bit of a movie in Oram's head, like none of it's real. He can't process that. A true leader in that position is assessing every situation in real time with real presence, no matter how fantastical it is, and they will make decisions on behalf of the crew. Oram's overwhelmed by it.

So when this figure approaches with a flare and scares off the Aliens and says, "Come with me," that's just a part of the movie in his head, like he hasn't ▶

4 /

5 /

▶ woken up yet. There's a genuine psychological break that happens in Oram, and it takes him some time before he can even find himself in the present, much less mourn the state of the expedition.

Tell us about working with your director, Ridley Scott.
Certainly for my generation, he occupies a sphere in the cinematic world like very few others. Working with Ridley has been one of the more extraordinary experiences I've had as an actor, because his creative engine is on all the time, and it's fascinating. He has this entire universe in his head, and it's very clear how it works to him. When he has that capacity and then chooses to collaborate with you and let you find your way into it, it's immensely rewarding because you know he's after something badass.

It's a one-of-a-kind opportunity, and I'm an actor who's had a great many phenomenal opportunities and a real embarrassment of riches. To be able to be a part of this is

moving to me, because these are movies I grew up with. I kept texting my high school friends saying, "Do you believe this? I'm in an *Alien* movie, man!" I have found Ridley to be an absolutely inspiring creative collaborator, and I feel privileged and blessed.

Did you work much with the stunts team?
I did, very briefly. Oram's reaction to most of what's happening is to hide, so I didn't have to do a lot of the action stuff. There is one sequence when he finally grows a pair and gets to take some vengeance. Then I got to talk to the tough guys.

What are your stand-out impressions from being on set?
It's awesome. You can't imagine some of the stuff that you see on a film like this, and the scale of it. Some of my favorite days were walking through the creature shop with my son, and getting to see them put together these Aliens and the craftsmanship that goes into it. I'm in awe of the design elements.

How would you describe the Aliens? What makes them unique?
Their intelligence is one thing that makes them unique, and their physiology. Ridley's really interested in biology himself, and so all of the various components that go into the Alien are things that he drew upon from nature. So while there is something otherworldly about it, there's something very familiar about it as well.

What are audiences going to experience, watching this movie?
I hope, like so many of the other *Alien* films, they'll experience an ungodly amount of tension. There's no question that we start off on our expedition with high hopes. At the first moment, within probably a minute or two, Daniels, says, "Stop," because she just wants to hear something, which is the sound of nothing. But from that moment on, they should be gripped with fear for the next two hours. I think they'll get their money's worth and then some. ●

5 / Oram tries to mentally process the discoveries he and his crew make on the planet

6 / Oram's strict Pentecostal religious background means he feels it's providence that he becomes the *Covenant*'s leader

DANNY MCBRIDE AS
TENNESSEE

Danny McBride talks about playing Tennessee, the salt-of-the-Earth pilot who will risk everything to save those he cares about...

Alien: Covenant Collector's Edition: How does it feel to be part of *Alien: Covenant*?
Danny McBride: It feels incredible to be a part of this film. *Alien* is the definitive sci-fi horror movie – no one has come close to touching on space and aliens quite the way Ridley has. So it's incredible to be a part of a franchise like that.

Can you introduce us to the character that you play? Who is Tennessee and how does he fit into the group?
I play Tennessee and he is the pilot of the *Covenant*. It's a colonization ship filled with couples, and my wife, Faris, played by Amy Seimetz, is the other pilot. We work together, and go off into space together.

Tennessee and Faris are the salt of the earth. They're surrounded by scientists, doctors and engineers, and Faris and Tennessee are just down-at-home, good people. They're a little different from the crew around them. They're a little lighter.

Tennessee has a special bond with Daniels. How do you see that connection?

Tennessee and Faris were friends with Daniels and her husband, Jacob, before we even left on the ship. So I think there's a bond that begins before this mission has engaged.

> "
> ## *Alien: Covenant* is a dark, dark story...
> "

Can you set up the differences for us between Oram and Tennessee?
As soon as it becomes apparent that the captain of the ship has passed, there is a moment where the crew's looking for guidance as to where to go next, and Oram's next in line. Oram has a very different way of leading than Jacob. Jacob was much loved and Oram gets off to a rocky start. He's a little more methodical, and he doesn't want to take the time to put Jacob to rest in a respectful manner. So that rubs a lot of people up the wrong way, especially Tennessee, who was very good friends with Jacob.

When the others go down in the Lander, does it feel like Tennessee's being left out of a great adventure?
When the crew decides to explore where the signal came from and Tennessee is left on the ship, it definitely feels like he's missing all the fun. He's stuck in the ship with Upworth and Ricks, who don't have the greatest personalities. They're a little stiff, and it looks like all the action and excitement is going to be happening down on the planet.

So Tennessee feels powerless?
One of the things I thought was most interesting about the script was the fact that the ship was filled with couples. And so instantly, it raises the stakes of the horror. It's not only about your own survival, but it's about the survival of the person you came there with, your husband or your wife. So when the action starts going on down on the planet, there's the horror they're going through, but then there's the horror for the people on board the ship that are left kind of helpless, just having to listen to their significant others and friends being ravaged.

▶

2 /

▶ **And then there's the transmission that Daniels has to make to you, telling you what's happened. How did you find acting that?**
Tennessee gets some very bad news on the ship, but he has to still stay in command of the ship and keep his head in the game. It was fun trying to tackle something like that.

Even the way Ridley shot it was really cool and inventive, and I knew that if I blew it, he could still make it seem cool, because he could just have it all happen off-camera.

How does it feel playing this cowboy, who ignores the repercussions to do what's right?
Whereas Oram is all about the mission, Tennessee is definitely about the people he cares for. He'll do whatever it takes to save them, and against the better judgment of the other crewmembers, he decides that it's worth risking the entire mission to get closer to the people on the planet and try to figure out what they need.

What did you like most about the script for *Alien: Covenant*?
What I really loved about this script was it was more of a straight horror. The moment you start to read it, it gets off to a dark start and the feeling of dread is overwhelming. It's just one bad choice after the next, and you see everyone get picked

off one after the other. It really reminded me of the first *Alien* film. I got the script and breezed right through it – I couldn't put it down. I was so stoked to see what happened, and it's a dark, dark story. The horror in it is what I think people are going to really respond to.

This is your first film working with Ridley. What are your impressions of working with him?
I loved working with him – he's great, he's got boundless energy. He's so passionate and excited about what we're doing, and as the guy who helmed the first *Alien*, it's awesome just to hear the stories about what those guys went through and what he was thinking when he was making that film. To be making something that's in those footsteps... it's cool.

What was it like to work with Michael Fassbender?
I have always been a fan of Michael Fassbender, and I thought his performance as David was pretty incredible. It was one of my favorite parts. So it was wild to walk onto the set of this and to be doing scenes with him. It was very difficult actually, because I've never acted with anyone who's playing an android in a movie before, so you're delivering lines to them and he's just looking

at you deadpan, not reacting to anything you're saying. That would make me laugh a lot, so I had to stop looking at him when I would talk to him, and then I could feel like he was kind of zeroing in on me, just staring at me with android eyes. So I never look at Fassbender in any of the scenes I'm in with him.

And what's it like working with Katherine Waterston?
Katherine's incredible. I think she's a perfect choice to pick up what Sigourney [Weaver] laid down. She's great, she's nice to work with and her dedication is incredible.

Tell us about your work with Connor O'Sullivan and the Creatures guys. Do you come across the Aliens much?
I have come across the Alien, the big boy, and I was surprised that the Alien was really here with us. It wasn't like you're running away

1 / Tennessee at the controls of the ship

2 / Tennessee tries to cope as he learns that his wife and friends are in grave danger

3 / A view of the *Covenant*, which Tennessee pilots

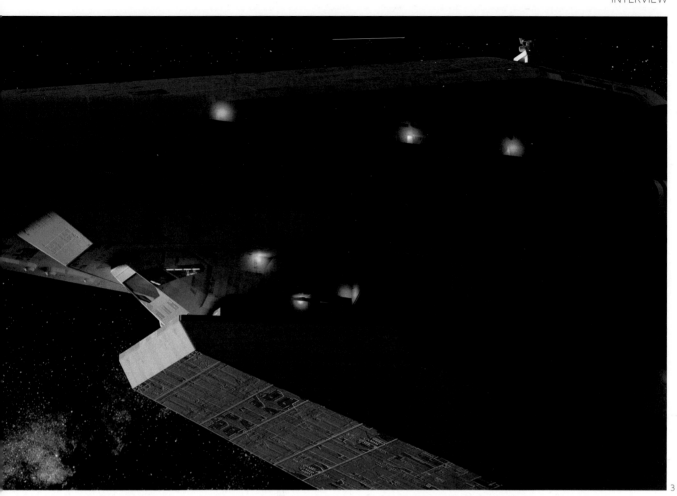

from a tennis ball. It was scary being in the scene, and it's dark and you see the door open up and it's just like, "Oh, there he is." It was pretty awesome. [*Laughs*]

How did you feel about Chris Seagers' sets?
The sets are incredible. I love the aesthetic of what this spaceship looks like – everything from the terraforming bay to all the construction equipment. It's just mind-blowing. The fact that we're in these spaceships for real... The cockpit of the *Covenant* was the first set I walked onto, and as soon as you look down the circular hallways, it feels like it's an *Alien* movie right away.

Why do you think the *Alien* movies have been able to stand the test of time?
Even when you watch the first *Alien* movie, the technology and the look of it still holds up. It doesn't look

like a dated science fiction movie. Ridley's always guessing what is to come, as opposed to making it based on what's here now. With everything from the Landers to the weird technology we have on the ship, he's always explaining how NASA or someone's working on a version of this now. So his mind just seems to be tapped into what's down the road, and I think that's maybe why *Alien* ages so well – because he knew where it was all heading.

What makes the Aliens in the *Alien* films so terrifying?
In the same way that *Jaws* terrified everyone about being in the ocean, *Alien* definitely has terrified everyone about having a foreign parasite in your stomach that could rip out of you at any moment! It's horrifying to think about – something using you as a nest and then discarding you in such a disgusting way.

Can you tell fans why they're going to love *Alien: Covenant*?
Fans are going to love *Alien: Covenant* because it's scary as shit. It's a straight horror film, and I think it's something that everyone's been waiting for since the original *Alien* movie, where you're seeing aliens and spaceships and you're scared out of your pants. That's what we've delivered here, I think.

What's your favorite moment from any *Alien* movie?
I think Bill Paxton [as Private Hudson in *Aliens*] is one of my favorite characters in any *Alien* movie. His epic monologue about "game over" is probably my favorite scene in any *Alien* film.

What would be your weapon of choice to fight an alien with?
Shotgun. That's what I chose in this film. I was shown weapons, and they asked, "What do you want?" I picked up the sawn-off shotgun. ●

CONCEPT ART - THE LANDER
The Lander is the *Covenant* crew's
means of getting down to the planet,
and their only way back...

AMY SEIMETZ AS
FARIS

Amy Seimetz plays Faris, the pilot who's forced into an impossible and terrifying situation…

Alien: Covenant Official Collector's Edition: Tell us about the character you play in Alien: Covenant?

Amy Seimetz: I play Faris, and I'm a pilot aboard the *Covenant*. I'm married to Tennessee, played by Danny McBride. We're both pilots, but apparently I'm the better pilot, which is why they send me down on the Lander to go explore this new planet that we find out there.

Can you tell us about Faris' relationship with Tennessee?
Danny McBride and I came up with a dynamic which means I have to match his humor, which is very hard! I think there's a mutual respect on both sides for Tennessee and Faris, because they're both pilots. Ridley said he believes they met in flight school and in a way their relationship developed because they were so competitive.

The new captain, Oram, gets off to a bumpy start with the crew, and perhaps Faris and Tennessee in particular…
When the shockwave hits the ship and we all violently wake up, we lose our captain, played by James Franco. It's very upsetting to us, because we were all friends

before, so losing our captain is heartbreaking. Tennessee and myself, Faris, were particularly close to the captain and his wife Daniels, and that's a big loss for us. I think we want to pay respect to the captain, not just personally, but also because he was a great captain. So when Oram is trying to take over and assert his power, we think it's too soon.

> **"**
> **Faris has a very heartbreaking decision to make…**
> **"**

Faris is described in the script as easygoing and likeable, but there's also a 'getting the job done' quality about her too.
Hopefully in the editing that will come through [laughs]. She's upbeat, but in the way that you always want your crew to feel good about what they're doing. So she's not upbeat to the point of being naïve or dumb, but her M.O. is about having a good attitude while you're doing some of these very difficult missions.

Not panicking and being afraid, until the point when she can't control that. But I think that's her. She's strong and upbeat, but she gets the job done.

When the crew pick up the strange signal, Oram chooses to head toward the new planet. What's Faris' perspective on that?
We're in the middle of space where we've been led to believe through all our research that there's no human life. So seeing a signal, or any sort of human form in the middle of outer space is shocking for everyone. In the military, if you get a transmission from somebody that seems to be in need of help, it's protocol to go and help.

It's complicated, because you get on a ship and you have this mission, these blinders on and this is the mission at hand. So it's a bit of a curveball, but for Faris at least, she's a pilot, and she likes exploring. So I think the idea of going off course is exciting to her.

Faris is left behind to work on the Lander while things go badly for the rest of the crew. Faris can only hear fragments of things going wrong. Is there a special kind of ▶

2 /

terror in hearing these things, but being powerless to help?

That's the way Ridley planned it – we filmed in New Zealand and it was just me underneath the Lander. We prerecorded all the calm stuff, so while I was by myself, I was able to hear these terrifying snippets, in and out of my earpiece, and react to that. Faris doesn't know what's going on – they sound confused, and the comm is breaking up, so there's just snippets of information. You can tell everyone's scared and it's really eerie, but that was very effective performance-wise, for us to hear everything and react to it.

Karine takes the infected Ledward back to the Lander and we see immediately the difference between Karine and Faris. Karine's hands-on, while Faris does everything to avoid infection.

It's not Faris' proudest moment, is it? But to defend Faris, while some would say she is cowardly, I would argue she's not. The crew are all trained in so many different areas in order to be part of the crew, including medically.

Faris' choice to put on the gloves and stay distant is really more about the fact that if they're infected, then she doesn't want to get infected, not just selfishly, but so it doesn't spread to the entire

1 / Faris is left with the Lander as the rest of the crew explores the planet

2 / Faris is shocked to hear the horrors her crewmates are experiencing

3 / Faris' cautious approach contrasts with Karine's compassion

4 / Faris arms herself to face down the Neomorph

crew. Faris goes immediately into medical protocol, because those rules are there for a reason. Just because one man's down, you don't want to infect everyone. That would ruin the entire mission. Even though Karine is her friend and is obviously in danger, Faris is trying to help, and quarantines the situation.

Tell us about Ledward and the Neomorph birth.

We haven't shot it yet, but I think it's going to be quite terrifying. Benjamin Rigby who plays Ledward is a very good actor, and I saw the make-up tests and it's disgusting!

Faris decides she must leave Karine to care for Ledward, and

locks the door. How awful is it to see her friend and know she can't let her out?

It's awful. She realizes that this is going horribly wrong, and sees how absolutely horrific this could be, not just for Karine and Ledward, but for the entire crew. It's the sound decision to try to quarantine them off so that it doesn't get any worse than that. Faris has a very heartbreaking decision to make, but it's a necessary decision in order to further the mission.

How do you see Faris' heroic, horrifying battle with the Neomorph?

I think it's instinct. Faris isn't just a pilot – the crew have been trained in different areas, and part

4 /

of that includes some military training, because we need to know how to defend ourselves going into these situations. So I think part of that is kicking into instinctual mode of, "I need to defend this mission, and kill this thing that's obviously killing our crew." Faris has never seen anything like the Neomorph before, so she's snapping into fighting mode, but also not knowing how to deal with something that she's never seen before.

How suspenseful will the finished movie be?
It's Ridley Scott, so of course you have the promise of incredible visuals and a story that's exactly executed. He's just so precise. I think it's going to be very

terrifying, just in the way we've been shooting it and the realness of the interactions with everyone, and the reactions that we're getting from the cast to the situation. It's very human and terrifying.

This is your first film with Ridley. What are your impressions of him?
I direct as well, so I always feel like I'm a spy coming onto these sets, and what an amazing set to be a spy on! I absorb everything that Ridley does. He's incredibly precise and knows everything he wants before we're on set. You can explore your character, but you have that safety net of such a seasoned and obviously iconic and brilliant director who's got your back. All you can do is enhance

the movie, but he's not going to let you screw it up [laughs].

Ridley has a long history with strong women characters such as Faris. How does it feel to be a part of that legacy?
It's incredible. I think what's fun is just, even in his demeanor toward women on set, everyone's an equal. So it's something I don't necessarily think about, because he's not reminding me that I'm a woman. I think it's really cool to have so many women who actually affect the narrative and are active characters in Ridley's films, and that's really exciting to me.

How does it feel to be a part of this legacy, especially with Ridley Scott?
I just feel like I have to have a set of new life goals, because I've surpassed my own. It's definitely surreal to be emailing home and saying, "I can't get to this until I'm done shooting with Sir Ridley." ●

CARMEN EJOGO AS
KARINE

Carmen Ejogo plays Karine, the *Covenant*'s biologist, whose
sense of compassion leads her into grave danger...

Alien: Covenant Official
Collector's Edition:
Can you introduce us
to your character?
Carmen Ejogo: I play Karine,
and I'm the biologist on board
the *Covenant*. I'm also the wife
of Oram, who happens to be
second-in-command until fateful
events put him in charge of the
Covenant.

**How do those events affect
your character?**
Oram is essentially the second-in-
command unless anything were
to happen to the captain, played
by James Franco. Suddenly, Oram
finds himself filling those boots,
which is a mixed blessing for
Karine in some ways.

It's absolutely what Oram
believed was his destiny. He's very
much a man of faith, and he felt
that the only reason he wasn't
given that position in the first
place was *because* he was a man
of faith, and that it might be some
kind of moral conflict for him.
He feels ready for it. He's capable
of it, but it also then requires
another level of almost babysitting
of Oram by Karine, because he's
struggling with a lot of existential
crises and constant insecurity.
Karine's really the backbone that

keeps Oram feeling level and
confident enough to take on
the position.

**After receiving a strange signal,
Oram decides to change course
towards a new planet. Not
everyone agrees with him. How
does that play out for Karine?**
Daniels feels it's a bad idea to
go away from the original plan,

> **"
> Karine's really
> the backbone
> that keeps Oram
> feeling level.
> "**

which was to go back into hyper-
sleep and travel on to this other
planet we'd set our minds on, but
there are advantages to taking
this idea up that Oram presents
to the group. The thing with
Oram is that it's not really *what*
he's saying; it's *how* he says it
that's the problem. I think the
idea of visiting this planet is not
necessarily a bad one, it's just
not presented in the right way.
So it's a little bit of a conflict for
my character as to whether it's a

good idea or a bad one. Being the
loyal wife that I am and seeing
the majority of the crew thinks it's
probably a good idea to try this
new option out, I end up going
with the flow.

**What happens when they
land there?**
It's not long into the journey
that we start to do the thing that
you should never do in a horror
film [*laughs*], which is we start
to go our separate ways. My
motivation is a good one, in that
I see that there is an opportunity
to do tests that would help us
determine if this is a good place
for us to colonize. So I take one
of the soldiers along with me, and
we embark on a journey deep into
this landscape, but it very quickly
starts to seem odd.

There are no birds. There's
flora, but no fauna. It's clear that
things are amiss. So the decision
to go our separate ways is maybe
not the wisest, particularly to go
with Private Ledward, who has
a tendency to venture off on his
own. It's the worst thing one can
do when you're not sure what
you're dealing with on the ground,
literally. Sure enough, the planet is
rife with matter that we are really
not familiar with, and it's the

beginning of the end [*laughs*] for many of us.

Once they're in Medbay, things go from bad to worse. Why do you think Karine stays?
There's something about Karine which I think is what Oram fell in love with and is consistently evident in the movie, and it's a degree of compassion. It's the thing that keeps Karine with Ledward even in the most disturbing of moments. She recognizes somebody that needs support, unlike Faris, who is a survivor in a very different kind of way and recognizes that she needs to get out of there and save herself.

Once in Medbay, it's quite clear that we're dealing with things that

1 / Biologist Karine initially feels a sense of wonder on landing on the planet

2 / Karine faces a fight for her life when her sense of compassion leads her into grave danger

3 / Karine tries to comfort the doomed Ledward (Benjamin Rigby)

are above and beyond anything we've handled before. I think there's a moment for Karine when she recognizes the futility of trying to continue to help, and that's when things get extremely stressful and anxious.

I think it's going to be the first moment in the movie for the audience that they are really reminded of the dread that we come to associate with the *Alien* movies. It's not that we've met any mysterious lifeform as yet, but you can sense that something is afoot that is going to be so dreadful and so out of our understanding that it will be horrifying.

So in Medbay, Karine meets a Neomorph. How terrifying is that?
It's not long after being in Medbay

that we realize Ledward is really in a condition that neither of us, neither I nor Faris, can handle. Faris takes the cowardly way out [*laughs*] and goes off to find help and locks me in. I try to remain as composed as possible, but there comes a point where Ledward is almost becoming beast-like in his agony, and in that moment, he gives birth to a Neomorph.

It's a really horrifying thing to witness, even as an actress in the room knowing that you're working with actors and special effects. It was still such a visceral moment for all of us, that it had me getting emotional in a way I wasn't really anticipating, which was great and hopefully was caught on camera. It's also testament to the work of the

special effects unit, because they've really created something that is a wonderful homage to the aliens of the original movie and the H.R. Giger aesthetic that we've come to know and associate with that lifeform. But it also had aspects to it that were somewhat unusual and quite new that I saw.

It all comes full circle in that moment when you meet the Neomorph for the first time. Karine has no idea what it is, and it's the mystery of it in that moment that I think is most palpable and powerful. It's not like being confronted with a tiger, where you have a sense of what's coming next. This thing is really quite small when it's born, although it grows rapidly in front of her, which is already quite

confounding, but also a mystery. It appears almost cute in a way, but there's something ominous and unknown about it, which makes it really terrifying.

What have been your most memorable experiences making the movie?
For me, Medbay was really remarkable. I never knew that amount of blood could adorn a set [*laughs*], but I'm really drowning in it from beginning to end, which was quite an experience. It'll either be my finest moment on camera or my worst [*laughs*]. I'm not sure yet, but it was certainly a new experience for me.

The energy that Ridley has, has been quite amazing to watch. This is a man who has had a really

astonishingly long and illustrious career, and he still seems to come to it with the same level of energy, inspiration and clarity of vision that I expect he had on the first *Alien*. I feel very lucky that I had a chance to experience that.

How does it feel to be part of the *Alien* legacy?
I grew up a fan of horror films, psychological horror mostly, and I think this is the epitome of that genre. There's an intellectualism that comes with the gruesome stuff, which I really appreciate. And there is also an interesting exploration of science and God and existential questions that are totally up my street. So I couldn't have wished for a better franchise to be part of. ●

BENJAMIN RIGBY AS
LEDWARD

We talk to **Benjamin Rigby,** who plays Ledward, the soldier
whose mis-step endangers the whole mission...

Alien: Covenant Official Collector's Edition: What is it about the *Alien* movies that have such a grip on us?
Benjamin Rigby: They definitely prey on our fears. I'd say what makes them so seminal is probably that the original *Alien* came about at a time when everyone had started to take an interest in space. It was only ten years after the moon landing, and then Bowie started making music about space and everyone started looking up and thinking, "Oh, maybe we're not alone." So I think that absolutely scares people, thinking that maybe we're not alone. And to be on a ship in the middle of nowhere and have something that's completely alien, pun intended, come onto the ship would be pretty terrifying [*laughs*].

How would you describe the aliens from the *Alien* films? Why are they so unique?
I'd say what makes them unique is they were originally designed by H.R. Giger, and that's awesome. You'd never seen something like that before, especially on film. You'd seen it in architecture and other things, but those shapes and lines and the character that

comes from that is mortifying. I'd say what makes them so unique is that they're Ridley's as well. He storyboards everything, and that's exceptional, but if you go into the creature workshop, they're working intricately on these monsters, and they're true artists.

"
It's my first Alien birth, definitely, but not my first death.
"

Did you ever have nightmares or favorite moments caused by the *Alien* franchise?
Nightmares, no, but I'm going to be really banal here and say the chestburster scene is probably my favorite scene. But after this film, I'd say I'll have my own death memories from *Alien* [*laughs*].

How did it feel to be cast in *Alien: Covenant*?
It was crazy. To get that phone call, you think it's going to be for something really small, and they say that you're in a Ridley Scott

movie and it's like, "What?" I genuinely thought I'd had a brain aneurysm when I got the phone call, and I didn't sleep properly for a week. So if that's telling, then it's pretty special. I start to pinch myself every day to remind myself that I'm doing this, hoping I'm not cut out of the film, because that would just be horrible.

Can you tell us about your character, Ledward?
Private Ledward's part of the expedition team. He's in the Army, so, essentially, when we go to the planet, he works as security for the biologists and other crewmembers of the ship. Ledward's a bit careless. He's oblivious to a lot of the stuff that's going on, so much so that he wanders off and has a cigarette and stuff goes crazy for him.

Things start off rough for the expedition, as Faris tries to steer the Lander through intense weather to land on the planet.
The Lander's a different ship from the *Covenant*, so we detach from the *Covenant*, but we have to go through this crazy storm. What we're about to film is going through that storm. It's pretty hectic, and then it's smooth sailing for at least a little while, ▶

▶ but then we land on the water on this amazing planet. They told us, "Pretend that it's beautiful and ominous and amazing," but we didn't have to do any acting, because New Zealand, where we filmed, was ridiculously beautiful!

Danger soon threatens Ledward, doesn't it?
Ledward doesn't really know what's going on – he's a bit too cool. He wanders off to have a cigarette, and his foot brushes up against this egg sac. Motes fly in front of him, and he just blows a smoke ring around them. Then there's a microscopic view of this high form of intelligence that goes into his ear, and he doesn't really notice, at least at first. This thing starts growing inside him, and it's restricting his breathing and heartbeat and he's sweating profusely and gasping for air, but Karine's trying to take care of him. She does as good a job as she can to get him back to the Lander and call on the comms to get help.

Once they're back in Medbay, Ledward's convulsing and spraying blood everywhere, is that right?
I'd say vomiting blood more than spraying. They've got this vomit rig that projectile-vomits, and it's pretty awesome. It's scary and it's going to be pretty crazy to see against the white of Medbay, but we're yet to shoot that. It's going to be very intense, but I like doing that kind of thing.

What is the Neomorph?
That's the alien that's been gestating inside of me and it comes out through my back and starts the whole process of killing people [*laughs*].

So is this is the first Alien birth for you, as an actor?
It's the first Alien birth, definitely, but not my first death. There was a period where producers just cast me in dead roles. There was about a year where it was like, "We want you naked or dead or both," and this is no exception [*laughs*].

2 /

Do you think *Alien: Covenant* will keep audiences on the edge of their seats?
Alien: Covenant will definitely keep you on the edge of your seat. I can guarantee that. It kept me on the edge of my seat, reading it. Maybe I'm biased because I'm in it, but there are a lot of twists and turns, and a lot of great characters that you really care for that you don't want to see hurt or in danger. I think that's the essence of it – there's a part of all of us in these characters.

What are your impressions of working with Ridley Scott?
He's awesome. He's so direct, and knows exactly what he wants, so he can just say one small thing, and it will give you such a scope of what you're supposed to be doing in that scene. He likes you to come up with a lot of your ideas as well, which was really freeing, coming into this. You don't have any restrictions, and from the script, you have a pretty good idea of the character that you're playing as well.

3 /

He's pretty hands-on, and in terms of set design and visual effects, it's all so amazing. So you walk onto set and you're just like, "Wow, the work's done for me." You get so used to doing theater or independent film and having to create a world for yourself, but with this film I feel completely at ease, and Ridley guides you in such a great way.

There was a moment in New Zealand where Carmen [Ejogo] and I had to block [rehearse the movements the characters make] through me walking behind her, and she wanted to know the steps of what we wanted to do. So I fell down on this beach in the middle of nowhere and Ridley picked me up and ran with me on the beach. I was thinking, "This 78-year-old guy, a living legend, is running

with me on the beach, and it's crazy!" He's really hands-on and knows exactly what he wants. He's mega-direct, and I really like that.

Tell us about working with this great cast.
Carmen Ejogo and I have a lot of scenes together, so it's been lovely to have this bond together. She's so nurturing and lovely and really motherly in a way, and I think that's why we were cast in these roles, because my character's really embarrassed about being sick and she has this beautiful nurturing quality. Billy Crudup's great and so funny, as is Danny McBride. Katherine Waterston is awesome, and Amy Seimetz. Everyone's great, and I'm really blessed to be amongst this cast.

How has it been working with the visual effects team?
I'd never had to do prosthetics before, so it's pretty cool seeing how it's all done and sitting in a make-up chair for hours waiting to see what happens at the end. It's just transformational. The Creatures department, in collaboration with the visual effects team, are on point. They know exactly what they're doing. I haven't seen people work like that before.

What scares you more? Being trapped in space with an Alien, or experiencing the birth of an Alien from your insides?
Is there an Option C? They're both pretty grueling. I'm going to have to say an Alien birth from my insides, because that's what I have to go through anyway [laughs]. ●

1 / Ledward bears the signs of being infected by the Neomorph spores

2 / The effects of Ledward's infection begin to make themselves felt...

3 / The agonising birth of the Neomorph begins, as Faris (Amy Seimetz) and Karine (Carmen Ejogo) try in vain to help Ledward

CONCEPT ART –
EXPLORING THE PLANET
The *Covenant* crew explore
the mysterious yet eerily
silent planet. But hidden
dangers lie in store...

1/

2/

1/ The planet's majestic landscape

2/ The *Covenant* landing party approaches the forest

3/ The crashed Engineers' Juggernaut

ALIEN
WORLDS

<u>Alien: Covenant</u> takes audiences to unfamiliar and terrifying places. The
task of creating those amazing sets falls to Production Designer

*A*lien Covenant: Official Collector's Edition: How did you get involved with *Alien Covenant*?

Chris Seagers: I had a little bit of history, as I had spent the last 10 to 12 years working with Tony [Scott, Ridley's late brother and fellow director], and I think Ridley and the producers were looking for somebody to come in and help out. I flew in to see Ridley around June and I suppose I was technically part of the family group.

Did you have a prior passion for the *Alien* franchise?
Absolutely. When you first get the phone call, it takes you back to when you were a teenager going to watch the original *Alien* and remembering those experiences, because you'd never seen anything like that before. It was so groundbreaking. And then suddenly to be offered a job like that was out of this world. So it was like getting goosebumps, and I was very, very nervous.

How did the aesthetic of the movie inform your design when you approached *Alien: Covenant*?
Although *Alien* was 35 years ago, things have moved on. Ridley didn't really want to get back to that, but for this particular journey there was a job for the ship and it was essentially to transport this group of people from A to B. The *Covenant* was very practical and utilitarian – it just did a job, which was to get people, equipment and everything needed to another planet to colonize it. So the basic brief was to get back to that *Alien* world of small spaces, dark corners and corridors.

Can you tell us about your first conversations with Ridley?
Those first conversations with Ridley were, essentially, that it was *Alien*, but that it would be tricky, because *Alien* was such an iconic movie and it set a style. We went around a bit at the beginning to try and find out how

we were going to do this, and I'd just finished a film [*Deepwater Horizon*] about an oil rig. I mentioned that a couple of times to Ridley, which he was interested in, because I would say these oil rigs are almost like spaceships. From the outside the oil rigs look like big tin cans, but inside they're full of technology, and they don't necessarily need people as there's just so much computer-driven stuff in them, so they're all automated.

On an oil rig you're in the middle of the ocean and you're sinking a seven and a half-inch pipe 18,000 feet and you're hitting a spot. It's the same as space technology, so it's all about guidance and navigation. It's all the same thing, and Ridley liked that. We started pulling a lot of references from that industrial world, and that's how we broad-stroked those early meetings.

Tell us about the process with Ridley.
The process normally goes that you shoot wide and we just go big. You go in and grab everything, and then you start to refine it down. There are usually elements from various sources that you start to mix together, and you go and create your own look from a mixture of other things. It's a fun process, because you just don't know where you're going to end up.

With the *Covenant* damaged at the outset of the film, what does that damage involve over the course of the story?
The damage is reflected in the Nursery and the Sleep Bay, with all the sleep pods coming loose and breaking and landing on the floor. That was pretty much the only area that we were seeing real damage in.

In order to get the movie done, we ended up having to use spaces over and over and over again. So the Sleep Bay became the Nursery, for instance – everything turned into two or three sets. We had to do a lot of physical mechanics in there, dropping these enormous pods, which turned out ▶

to be quite a challenge, because everything was so heavy. The whole Nursery and the Sleep Bay were all on airbags, in order to get that physical movement.

How has it been working with an Australian crew on this movie?
Working with the Australian crew has been fantastic. When we first talked about it, having not worked here, I must admit I was a little nervous. It wasn't necessarily nervousness because you couldn't do it. It's just that doing space and spaceships are very different, and it's not like doing a [period movie] or something where you just put a bit of brown paint on and you can cover it up. Especially with Ridley, because Ridley loves the layers and detail, so it had to have that detail in small spaces where you have electricians, carpenters, painters, set decorators, all these people. Everybody's in small spaces. It just doesn't work, so it's all about timing.

I've had a supervising art director, Ian Gracie, who's been fantastic at organizing all of that, which has been a minefield. But somehow we've come through it and managed to pull it all together. So it's been very good.

This film is more about the Aliens and cat and mouse chases. Did that help shape your approach to designing the sets?
We are essentially making a horror movie, and that has influenced a lot of the spaces: narrow corridors, long corridors, lots of tight spaces and dark spaces... But if you're going to go dark, you don't want to go black.

The way that we've approached the design of it was to try and make sure that we didn't have a lot of sharp corners. We rounded off all the corners so that they caught the light and it gave you the depth, and giving the suggestion that there were other things going on. You wouldn't necessarily see it all, but it wasn't just black holes. That was probably the biggest challenge. There were a lot of tricks we were playing so that it wasn't all totally black, because it could go black very quickly. ●

1 / The Xenomorph makes its appearance in the *Covenant*'s Terraforming Bay

2 / A model shot of the Lander

3 / A design model showing the Lander's ramp being deployed

4 / The Lander's cockpit and crew area

5 / A dead specimen in David's Lab

6 / The different stages of David's experiments

7 / An Alien head cross-section

8 / The White Room complete with 'David'

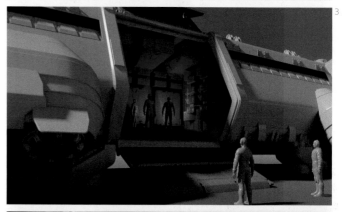

THE LANDER

The Lander was a little bit of a challenge, only because when it first comes down to the planet, we see it using a lot of [filmed] plates that we shot in New Zealand and then we ended up landing it on the bay at Milford Sound.

We needed a platform, a ramp, an archway and an engine for the crew to come out of in order to get some physical elements there, which we ended up building on the beach in Milford Sound in between the tides, which is quite interesting.

We also ended up building the entire Lander interior on a stage as a composite, but again, because of the whole entry into the atmosphere, Ridley wanted to have a quite violent motion on that.

We couldn't afford to rock the entire set, so we had to work out how we could split the cockpit off the rest of the set, then overnight connect it back in again so that it could continue shooting, because we ended up having to go from the loading bay up to the cockpit, down the corridor into Medbay, and that was all multi-camera shooting, done in one or two takes.

DAVID'S LAB

David's spaces – his lab, his chamber and the egg room – are in a corridor that leads you down underneath the Hall of Heads, and his chamber was essentially where you get an introduction to what David's been up to. You first think that maybe he's messing around in a good, experimental way, trying to do good. Then slowly you start to realize as you go down deeper into the lab that it's not necessarily all for the better.

7 /

6 /

8 /

THE WHITE ROOM

The white room was an interesting one, because Ridley wanted to make a little homage to 2001, and it was the birth of David. Ridley really wanted to get the Michelangelo 'David' in there, and it was a tricky one because it took him years to sculpt [*laughs*], and we had to do the whole thing in four weeks. We ended up calling the V&A [the Victoria & Albert Museum, in London], because we knew they had a replica of 'David'. We got a company in London to go in and scan it, and send us the file, and we ended up cutting him out of foam. Then our sculptors came in and refined it.

9 /

THE DREADNOUGHT

The Dreadnought designs were in the early *Alien* movies, although they only built small pieces of it. So we ended up tweaking and changing it a little bit, and construction methods have changed even in the last five years.

We ended up having to design it in such a way that we could shoot the nav chamber with the navigation chair in there. We could take all that out, and we then added all the desolation and the rubble for the crashed Juggernaut.

Ridley wanted to go back to the early *Alien* corridors, which were much smaller, and more organic and tactile. They are much more skeletal and have more of that Giger-esque look, so they're a lot scarier.

10 /

THE COVENANT BRIDGE

One of the big things with the *Covenant* Bridge was the overall size of it, and we did reference back to *Prometheus* for that, and also the *Nostromo* [from *Alien*], and we ended up somewhere in between the two. Ridley liked the whole idea that it had the feel of the inside of an aircraft.

We're so far in the future, but Ridley also wanted to make it very tactile for the actors, so that all the switches and dials worked. It needed around 1,500 circuits in there so that everything worked for the actors, because we were in there for so long.

11 /

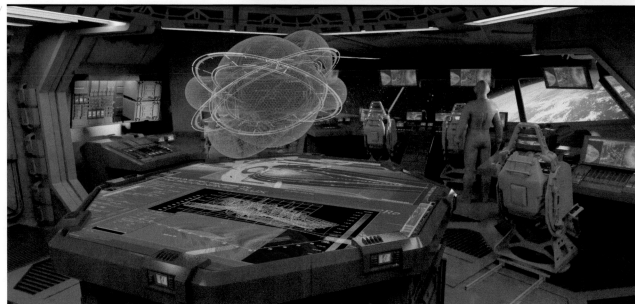

THE TERRAFORMING BAY

The Terraforming Bay was a very different space only because in our movie world it was one of four Terraforming Bays at the back of the ship, and they were like the trailers of the ship where they kept all the equipment, and that was Daniels' area.

In the end, for various reasons, we ended up just using the empty stage, which I believe they did in the original *Alien*. We covered the walls in aluminum foil and insulation felt to give it some shininess on the walls for that spacy feel, but it was just a great big empty space full of big equipment.

When you get into spaces that big, the money starts racking up, and it was tricky, because we ended up building just one of the trucks, as we couldn't afford to build two. We replicated the truck as a CG element, and then when the truck travels down the ramp going out the door, to make that door mechanical, these days you'd do it with CG, but we were in the Terraforming Bay for a number of days before we're seeing it closed. We just didn't have the money to build a real door, so we drew it all in digitally. It was 32 meters wide or eight meters high – we printed it all out on plywood and stuck it up, and it was a quarter of the price.

12 /

13 /

9 / Walter (Michael Fassbender) and Daniels (Katherine Waterston) explore the Engineers' Dreadnought

10 / The *Covenant* crew in the claustrophobic-feeling Bridge

11 / A concept design for the *Covenant*'s Bridge

12 / A suited performer as the Xenomorph on top of the Terraforming truck

13 / The Xenomorph makes its presence felt in the *Covenant*'s Terraforming Bay

NATHANIEL DEAN AS
HALLETT

Nathaniel Dean on playing Sergeant Tom Hallett, the military man who experiences whole new levels of pain and terror…

Alien Covenant Official Collector's Edition: How does it feel to be in an *Alien* movie?

Nathaniel Dean: First off, it's an honor to get the gig. The whole thing has been amazing. We got to Milford Sound, where we were location shooting, and I'll remember that day forever, where the Lander door comes down, and we're walking onto this planet to explore it. Michael [Fassbender] walked in front of me, and we're all rigged up with guns and everything, and I was just thinking, "I'm shooting an *Alien* film!" It's a real joy, but it's really hard work. They're long days, they're really arduous; it's a really physical film. Ridley asks a lot of you, but I like that pace. I like to let myself go, and scene after scene Ridley works very diligently and specifically. When you walk onto a set, generally the first take is *the* take, so you've got to come prepared. You've got to come with your A-game. I've just loved it.

How much of a difference does it make having real, practical effects and sets to work with?

In the original movie, just because of the budget, you didn't actually get to see the Alien that much. Sometimes I think that can be more terrifying. The way that Ridley works, it's a very practical set, so you're in quite a real world. There's very little CGI, so the Aliens are right there looking right at you, which is great.

Playing in a practical world, having these sets built – and the detail of these designs of the creature thanks to Connor O'Sullivan's work – as part of the world that you're playing in, means

> **"**
> **I hope it's as terrifying to watch as it was to act…**
> **"**

half the job is done for you. You're just reacting, and I think you do a lot of preparation at home where you're building up the back-story to your character and are daydreaming about, "What is this Alien going to be like?" To have it presented to you on the day is sublime.

Hallett and Sergeant Lope have an unique relationship…

My character, Hallett, is married to Lope. They've been married for quite a few years and they love each other. It's a very real thing.

I think it's really great that John [Logan, the screenwriter] and Ridley and the rest of the people developing this movie have put this relationship into space, because you would hope that with humanity in however many more years, [homophobia] isn't a thing; that people can just love each other, and that they're just humans. I think it's a great thing for them to be putting this [kind of relationship] into the *Alien* franchise. They're just good people who love each other. They just happen to be badass soldiers and good with M4 rifles.

How does Hallett deal with being on the mission?

The one thing with Hallett is he struggles with being in space, and it's a thing that I think he's managed to hide during the years of training. He does struggle with confined spaces. Hallett's looking forward to being on that planet, rather than being in a floating tin can.

After the captain dies, how does Hallett deal with events?

When Jacob dies in cryo-sleep, ▶

2 /

▶ it dismantles the leadership of the crew. Hallett's instant reaction is one of dissension, and I don't believe that he thinks Oram's got what it takes to be leading this crew. I'm pretty sure Hallett would think it would be Lope's job to take on that role.

One of the major worries would be that the equipment's failed and someone's just died, so what's to stop something else happening? I think this leads to Hallett having his own insecurities about space, like when they're coming in on the Lander and it's a pretty bumpy ride. He's losing a bit of faith in the equipment. We strap ourselves into this Lander and it's hairy – it's shaking, it's dropping 20 to 30 feet; it's crazy. Hallett's not coping with that. He tolerates space to a point, but this is the point where he wants to tap out. Lope's having a ball, and that's driving Hallett mad.

When the crew find the Dreadnought, Hallett's curiosity gets the better of him...
When we come across the Dreadnought, the whole crew know something's wrong. That moment where we see the mold and what looks like egg sacs... There's a natural reaction from everyone – "Maybe we shouldn't be here..." Lope wants to get out of there, and Hallett does as well, but he keeps on looking and unfortunately steps on something. Not that he knows it at that point, but things are not going to go well for him.

The crew races back to the Lander where things get even worse. Take us into the chaos of that moment.
Hallett gets sick really quickly. The Alien attaches itself to his bloodstream, to his internal organs. He's very disoriented, he's choking, he can't breathe and it's a massive struggle to move. It's desperate, and they all know that something is not right. Time's ticking fast for poor old Hallett...

What was it like filming the birth?
When the Alien comes out of Hallett's mouth, it's pretty extreme. It's basically ripping his whole head in half. It's not a normal way to give birth. [*Laughs*]

There are some moments where you've got to pinch yourself on set. You're on the ground, sitting there covered in blood, with this weird prosthetic thing in your mouth screaming for your life. Suddenly, you've got Ridley coming over, being so excited! I was tripping out, because Ridley was going, "All right, let's give birth to an Alien!" Like, "Let's do this!" Connor O'Sullivan was hanging over the top of me with a jerry can full of blood, which was sugary, syrupy stuff. That was the first part of it. The next part was this amazing head they made of me, which is a trip in itself, let alone seeing this thing come out of its jaw, and I'm making the sound for that Alien.

3 /

That went into my brain, forever. I haven't watched the scene yet, but I hope it's as terrifying to watch as it was to act.

Tell us about working with Connor O'Sullivan and the VFX team on these terrifying Aliens.
I walked into the VFX department and there was this moment where they put all this goop over me. It's quite a claustrophobic moment, just trying to breathe through your nose. The whole time, I was thinking, "What the hell am I doing getting my head molded?"

Connor sat me down and said, "Basically, this alien comes out of your mouth, dude." Not only that, they had a version of how it might come out of my mouth.

I had to sit very still for about an hour while they were color-matching my skin tone. Then in the background, there's my body with this Alien coming out of it and I'm trying to sit still, going, "Okay, get a grip." It's wonderful to see these artists and what they're creating, from a two-story-high head, to tiny little Aliens with hands, jaws and

eyes that move – the whole thing's been fantastic!

What scares you more? Being trapped in space, just you and the Alien, or the birth of an Alien from your insides?
Both things are terrifying. But having gone through it in this movie, I'd have to say that having an Alien within you ripping your face apart to escape is probably the most terrifying thing. The day I watched my fake head have that happen to it is a nightmare I will carry with me forever. [*Laughs*]

1 / Nathaniel Dean as Sergeant Tom Hallett steps out of the Lander to explore the planet

2 / Hallett's curiosity gets the better of him in the alien Dreadnought...

3 / Hallett starts to show the signs of Neomorph infection

DEMIÁN BICHIR AS
LOPE

Actor **Demián Bichir** plays Sergeant Lope, the soldier who has to face many horrors in order to protect the *Covenant* crew…

Alien: Covenant Official Collector's Edition: How does it feel to be part of the *Alien* legacy with Ridley Scott?

Demián Bechir: I never really think of the bigger picture or what any of that represents. I try not to think about the names or their background, because then you might enter a state of fear. I only think of everyone as a team, and when you think of Ridley Scott, that is one of those names you put on your Christmas list. So I'm glad that finally Santa Claus heard my prayers – that alone is a gift! It's a gift for you as an actor, because I wish I could have seen how Jules Verne worked, or Michelangelo, or any of those geniuses.

So when I have the chance to work with such a heavyweight in my time in the movie business, it's a real gift, because I pay attention and I just love to see them in action and see how they do what has made them famous. When you dream of doing science fiction, if you ever get that chance and you're lucky to be a part of it, you want to do it with the masters, and Ridley is without a doubt, the boss. I thought, 'This is payoff time!'

Can you introduce us to the character you play in *Alien: Covenant*?

I play Sergeant Lope, and I'm in charge of the military part of the mission. I have a small platoon, which might not be sufficient to deal with so many different unknown variables, but that's what we have. Our mission is to keep everyone safe, and we are trained for it and we will do our best to keep it that way.

> ## As an *Alien* fan, it's exciting to be in front of this iconic figure.

What is Lope's relationship with his second-in-command, Hallett?

This spaceship, the *Covenant*, is formed of couples, since we are on a colonizing mission, and Sergeant Hallett and Lope are a couple. We were really grateful when they chose us to be a part of this mission, because our relationship might cause some friction, not only because we are a couple and we love each other,

but also because he served as my subordinate. That would probably raise some eyebrows. Nevertheless, first and foremost, as well as being lovers or husbands, we are soldiers. We're soldiers and we're trained for that, and we take this mission seriously.

A lot of people on your team talk about how you named the platoon.

We call ourselves 'Perros Locos' – Crazy Dogs. I don't even know how that happened, but one day we became Crazy Dogs back in boot camp. We've been Perros Locos ever since [*laughs*].

Take us into the moment, from Lope's perspective, when it all goes wrong.

As they say, you have to prepare for anything, be ready for the worst and hope for the best, and sometimes the best gets affected by external events or agents that you probably weren't even aware of. So when we experience that first event where we lose our captain, that shakes everything and turns our plan upside down. We did not expect that, and in those situations you have to regroup, make the relationship tighter, get ready for the next new commander to call the shots, and ▶

then follow orders. That's a basic principle in the military. You're trained to obey.

Can you describe to us what happens when Hallett gets sick?
He's the first one that gets infected. We don't even know what's going on with him, right in front of our eyes, and that changes our game plan. It's particularly stressful and overwhelming when your loved ones get so sick, because you can't think clearly, but you have to. So that's a big challenge for all of us, because it's about survival from that point on.

I've never seen anything like it in my life. It's horrible. I don't think I've ever had any nightmare such as that. Not in my wildest nightmares could I imagine that that could happen to a human being, so it's triple scary. One, we don't know what it is. Two, we might all have it, and three, it's happening to the love of my life. That creates a bigger conflict.

Then David comes to save them?
David is a synthetic who seems friendly because he looks like

us. So we trust him and he helps us escape from that particular situation, and the only chance we have is to follow him. We're not even sure that David's telling the truth, or if we're walking into a bigger trap.

From your interactions with the Aliens so far, how is it seeing them in front of you for the first time?
First of all, as an actor, it's quite a challenge to imagine something that's not there, but also as an *Alien* fan, it's exciting to be in front of this iconic figure. It's probably the same feeling that I got when I first saw the Statue of Liberty, or other things that I've only seen in photos. When you're face to iconic face, it's exciting. It's one of those things that makes you happy as an actor.

What is it like working with Ridley Scott?
I think Ridley confirms that great masters make everything really easy, simple and loving. It's just a joy to confirm what you always imagined these big names would be like on set, and with you personally. He

turned out to be such a loving man and of course, savvy and smart, and he has more energy than all of us put together. He's always there and he's always ready. He broke his wrist, but nothing stops him. We all love him.

We had some one-on-one sessions that were really fulfilling and rich. Sometimes you work on films where you don't even rehearse or read or talk about the character with your director, and that's also fine. There are many ways of approaching the work and you're supposed to be ready to solve any problems under any circumstances, but to have the chance to have those sessions one-on-one with this man was an incredible part of the process.

Will this film have us on the edge of our seats?
Well, it has had me on the edge of my seat every day we've been shooting. It's a horror film that's really well told. I'm only putting the pieces together as we shoot – I'm imagining the different situations happening and how this master will cut them and put it together to make us suffer.

3 /

I can't wait to see this film. It's one of those films you are really eager to see cut together, because there are so many different things happening as we're shooting that there's going to be a lot of work afterwards, after we wrap this phase of the process.

What are your impressions of Chris Seagals and his team's sets?
We were talking about that just yesterday when we filmed in the Engineers' city for the first time. I didn't want to take a look beforehand... I could have peeked inside, but I wanted to hold off until it was the first time for the character, and it was very impressive. The sets make a big difference in your work as an actor. You need all those elements to be like that – colossal and monumental, not only in size, but in quality.

What do you think it is that continues to fascinate people about the *Alien* films?
The way they're made. You have to be a master to step into that territory over and over again and do it so precisely. That's what happens when the commander-in-chief is such a heavyweight like Ridley, because he gathers the best of the best in every department in every corner. So everywhere you look, you'll see only the best.

What would be your fondest memory or nightmare from *Alien: Covenant*?
[*Laughs*] I think one of the creepiest moments is when the little Neomorph comes out of the sergeant's mouth. That was pretty creepy, even though I saw the way it was made – but that was something. ●

4 /

ALEXANDER ENGLAND AS
ANKOR

Alexander England plays Ankor, the enthusiastic soldier whose optimism is soon tested by the unimaginable horrors he faces…

*A*lien: Covenant Official Collector's Edition: Tell us a little about your character, Ankor.
Alexander England: We're part of a security detail that's been contracted to protect the colonists. Private Ankor is one of the soldiers, and he's pretty happy just to be a part of it. There's an excitement to him – but that pretty quickly gets rained on by the events of the film.

When the team investigates the Dreadnought, how does Ankor feel about it?
I don't know if Ankor wished he could go in, but we're ordered to wait outside. It's unusual that you'd find an incredible vessel like that and no sign of anything around. I think that's when they take their guns off safety, and they're aware that something not quite right is happening. It's a sign of advanced alien life – that's exciting, and potentially threatening in and of itself.

Then we start getting reports through the earpiece that something's up with Ledward. So we start hotfooting it back, and then people start expiring, and it all falls apart for them very quickly.

How do the team cope when the Neomorph emerges?
I was lucky enough to be up close and personal when that Neomorph popped out of Hallett's head. The creature design is obviously a massive part of these films, and the Neomorphs have a distinct feeling and aesthetic as opposed to the Xenomorph, the big, black original. There's something cute about a little baby

> **"**
> **Ridley said dread is more interesting than terror in his opinion…**
> **"**

popping out of somewhere, even if it is someone's head! This little fawning creature comes out, and it's not necessarily threatening right there in and of itself, but they start to grow pretty quickly into horrifying, spiky beasts.

At that point, it's a matter of survival. I think there's the awareness that we might not survive, but that we're also

responsible for all those people on the *Covenant*. I think it's hard for them to come to terms with how it's all going so wrong.

Do you think the film will terrify audiences watching it?
The film is about tension. Ridley said dread is more interesting than terror in his opinion. You're aware that people are likely to start dying at some point, you just don't know when. So Ridley's created this story where for a long time you're waiting for a reveal. People like to be surprised, and I think at this point in the series, that suspense is important to keep people guessing.

How did you find the boot camp training you received?
I'm not sure what I was imagining, but it was a great chance for us to hang out together, and work as a team to build that kind of cohesion.

The weaponry is important too. John [Bowring] and his team have put together some really interesting weapons, but they're not so futuristic that they're not familiar. So, we've got the M4s – you pick one of those guns up, and you feel like a badass. There's no acting required! ●

LOCK AND LOAD

To take on a Xenomorph or Neomorph requires some serious firepower, and the man who arms the *Covenant* crew is head armorer John Bowring…

1

*A*lien: Covenant Official Collector's Edition: What does it involve, being a head armorer?
John Bowring: I look after all the firearms and replicas of firearms and associated equipment. The special effects and art department background I have has given me the ability to make the soft and hard replicas, and to understand the looks that we're after and the different film genres. I have a gunsmithing background way back in my dim, dark past too, which is where I get the ability to be able to manufacture and modify firearms to work with blank ammunition.

How did Ridley Scott describe to you what he needed?
When I first spoke to Ridley about the weapons, I'd thought that maybe we were after something more space age, but Ridley said he wanted weapons that were real. What we've done is come up with some fairly modern weapons, which we've modified slightly to take them a bit further into the future, and make them work for the roles they needed to perform.

Ridley has a very hands-on approach. Everything has to be passed under his eye before it goes on set. Originally, we thought maybe he would want something more military-looking, with a camouflage coloring similar to what you'd have with a military detachment. He wanted to downplay the military background of the personnel in this film, so he chose fairly austere colors of grays, blacks and some silver.

How do you balance realism and science fiction?
To make sure that the weapons work, we start with a real weapon as a base. It's too expensive to design something from the ground up. We then look at what we can do to enhance them to make them as we think they will be further into the future.

How did you prepare the actors to use the weapons?

I got in some specialist military personnel as well as me to train them. We trained them in what the military would do, and also informed them about the sorts of things which help keep them looking right in the film genre. What is perfect in the military world or the real world is not absolutely perfect for film.

Can you tell us about some of the weapons the characters use?
We were very lucky or privileged that we had decided we needed

1 / Previous Spread Daniels (Katherine Waterston) fights back against the Aliens with a 'bullpup' rifle

2 / Ankor (Alexander England) wields his M4 carbine as he runs into action followed by Rosenthal (Tess Haubrich)

two different types of weapons, and one of them was what's called a bullpup. A bullpup is a shorter weapon, because the action is moved back behind your hand. So the magazine sits behind the firer's hand and that allows the weapon to be made very short.

A company called Thales were able to supply us with seven rifles from their new production run for the Australian Army. They have the advantage that if you're using one hand, the weight is directly over the center of the hand. So

2 /

down the path of designing one. So we stepped a little bit ahead of the gun design there!

All the weapons have collapsing stocks, even the shotgun. If we reduced the length, we could make them much more easily handled by the stunt people and actors in confined areas.

We also added a lot of Picatinny rails [brackets to clamp accessories to], because there are a lot of dark scenes. Most of the weapons are equipped at some stage with a green laser and frequently with torches, because of the lighting effects that we can get with those. The torches were used for some of the internal scenes, where it's very dark and they've been selected by the DoP to give him the lighting he requires.

What's kept you busy on the film?
We had to make hard and soft versions of each weapon. So we manufacture all the stunt weapons, which generally have a hard, real version, and a hard, lightweight version that looks absolutely like the real one. Then we'll have a soft, flexible version, so that if we're using it in a high-energy stunt, it's not going to cut or hurt anyone, and can be reused. We also make sponge rubber pistols, because if a stuntman lands on a hard pistol in a holster, that's dangerous. So we do a real one, a hard light one and a sponge rubber one.

We normally have two of every blank-firing rifle, so if there's a stoppage or a breakage on set, we can replace the weapon without having to stop to replace the part. It's very important that we keep moving when things happen.

What would be your weapon of choice to fight an Alien?
I've got to say, a shotgun does take some beating. You can put in big, solid slugs, or you can put in small shot. So it's got a tremendous amount of knock-down power. The F90 with the grenade launcher is a hell of a lot of fun too – certainly the sort of thing you could hunt Aliens with. ●

that got used for the scenes where there was a lot of one-hand holding, but also one of them had to have a bayonet come out of the fore-end. So we had to design a new fore-end that would give enough room for the bayonet to slip down inside. Daniels uses that in a fight with the Alien.

In the scenes where Daniels has to dangle under the spacecraft, we chose to use the bullpup design, because the action's behind your hand. It's not like holding the weapon on one end and having

it work against you. You're actually just holding the weight. It makes it very easy for her to maneuver and fire, one-handed, plus it's fully automatic.

What kind of modifications have you made to the weapon designs?
On the F90s, we built a rail system for the front of them, which we had 3D printed, and that's something that may in future end up on these rifles. When I mentioned it to Lithgow Small Arms, they said they were already

**CONCEPT ART –
THE ENGINEERS' CITY**
The crew overlook the awe-inspiring
dead city of the Engineers...

ULI LATUKEFU AS
COLE

Uli Latukefu on playing Cole, the *Covenant* security team's most impulsive member...

Alien: Covenant Official Collector's Edition: Tell us about the dynamics of the *Covenant*'s security group.
Uli Latukefu: The dynamic of the team, under Hallett and Lope, is really quite family-orientated. The crew are a small group anyway. We don't get to see too much of the personalities, but overall the feel of the crew is that they are a tightly knit group of people.

How did you find the military training that you and the other actors playing the soldiers did?
We did a two-week boot camp, where we did a mixture of cross-training and weapons work, and learning how to use the guns under pressure, which was really tough and I don't mind not doing it again for a while. All that helps us build our character, and when we get to filming, we can throw it all away and muscle memory kicks in. It was harder than I thought. I don't know how soldiers do it. They're like supermen.

What would be your weapon of choice to fight an Alien with?
Any kind of gun with a grenade launcher on it, which is what I have in the movie, and I don't even end up using it [*laughs*]!

How did Ridley Scott go about shooting the first Alien battle scene?
Ridley's done a really amazing job shooting that sequence. He shot it so fast, considering the amount of logistics going into it – the fact that it's set in two different places, the Lander and out in the field. He knew what he wanted to do really early, planned out a lot of it and shot it. I'm surprised that we shot it that quickly, but it goes to show why he is who he is, because of that approach and his work ethic.

> "
> *Alien* makes the decision that the unknown is against us.
> "

Can you talk a bit about what happens when the team comes across David?
We just shot the scene where what's left of the team walks into the Hall of Heads, and it's amazing, just the scale of it. We walk into this room and David reveals himself. Immediately everyone goes, "Oh, Walter?" There's that comparison where we

realize [they're the same model], and then he, of course, explains what happened to Elizabeth Shaw. We're forced to trust him – we have no other option, being stuck on this planet. So we're at the mercy of this guy who we've just met, who comes across as quite genuine in wanting to help us, but it may turn out otherwise.

Let's talk about Ridley Scott and what it's like to work with him.
Ridley, for me – I don't know what it was like to work, say, 20 years ago, but he just reminds me of that style of filmmaking when film was around. He has an approach to his work that's extremely thorough, well-detailed, and extremely well-planned, and, for an actor, it's super-helpful. As much as you prepare yourself, you can come in and vibe and see what happens and trust in his direction. He's super-warm, super-friendly and super-funny. When I first got the job I knew who Ridley was, but I just wanted to Google him and see if I could find out something about him that we could have some sort of rapport about. Every single photo of Ridley, he has a really serious, stern-looking face, and I thought, "Great, no sense of humor." I like to joke around, and it turned out he has a great

▶

sense of humor. He's really, really
funny, and genuinely enjoys
creating the work that he does,
so it's been a joy. It's been such
a learning experience for me.
I've loved every minute of it.

**What was it like working with
Michael Fassbender?**
I mean, he's Michael Fassbender.
He's extremely professional, but
I wasn't too sure about how
you work with him [at first].
Someone like me is still quite
new to the industry, and working
opposite Michael could have been
intimidating. But I just found him
to be so open, welcoming and
encouraging of ideas. One time,
I suggested something to Michael
and he said, "Go for it. Do it. If
it's your instinct, do it." Coming
from someone like Michael, who's
had the amount of experience that
he has, it's encouraging, to say
the least.

How about Katherine Waterston?
Katherine has this natural, family,
team vibe-building personality
about her. One of the things she
suggested was that in the first
Alien, you see everybody come
together at the dinner table, which
builds up that family vibe, and she
suggested we should build on that.
It wasn't explicitly written in the
script, but we eventually did some
extra things that helped build
toward that feel for the film.

**Why do you think the *Alien*
movies have such a grip on us?**
I think the thing people find
interesting about the *Alien* films
and franchise is this curiosity we
have with exploring the unknown,
and I think because *Alien* presents
the idea of something out of the
unknown as threatening.

We don't even know whether
the unknown is for us or against
us, and quite clearly, *Alien* makes
the decision that the unknown is
against us. It's kind of grim, but
it's true. ●

1 / Uli Latufeku as Cole
explores the planet

2 / Cole is shocked
to encounter a Face-
Hugger

TESS HAUBRICH AS
ROSENTHAL

Tess Haubrich plays Rosenthal, the sole woman in the *Covenant*'s military squad...

*A*lien: Covenant Official Collector's Edition: Tell us a little about your character.
Tess Haubrich: My character, Rosenthal, is one of the security team on the ship. Ankor and Rosenthal have a bit of a thing going on. We think maybe our partners are asleep, because everyone else who's awake has coupled up except for us!

What makes the Aliens so scary?
I think the fact that they're eyeless scares me, as they don't have windows to the soul. Also, it's the way they progress so rapidly from juvenile to adult – I find that really scary. They're just terrifying to look at; and clever, very clever.

What are your fondest memories of the *Alien* franchise?
My fondest memory of *Alien* would have to be the first chest-burster scene. I think because the acting in that is so real, it's like they're not acting. Then, in *Prometheus*, with Elizabeth Shaw, realizing she's pregnant with the alien and that she has to cut it out, I thought that was amazing. Noomi Rapace's acting is everything in it.

What's it like being in such an iconic series?
When I found out, I was very

overwhelmed. I'd just had a baby, and didn't think I would get the part. It's been an amazing experience. Ridley's amazing to work for and it's just been very exciting. I'm very lucky.

How does Rosenthal deal with what the crew find on the planet?
Rosenthal is a little bit in shock, and when you're going through something that's so unknown and you don't know how you feel about

> **"**
> **I, being the only woman at boot camp, really had to show how strong I am.**
> **"**

it, you have a feeling it isn't a good thing to be doing. So they go to the Dreadnought that has all these bodies in it, like Pompeii, and there's death all around them.
My character doesn't really find the hologram [of Elizabeth Shaw], the hologram finds her, though it catches her by surprise, just randomly in the Dreadnought. I think it's exciting to find it, but it's all very distressing. Shaw doesn't

sound happy, so Rosenthal's impulse is to go back, but Oram, the captain, has said they have to investigate, and everyone else is interested.

What can audiences expect from *Alien: Covenant*?
When I first read the script, at the end my heart sank. I don't know if that's a huge giveaway, but yes, it got me. It's pretty damn scary – even to read it I got quite scared, and I'm very brave.

How did you find the boot camp?
We did all this fitness work and learned how to actually use the weapons and look like we know what we're doing. We did full military push-ups and I, being the only woman at boot camp, really had to show everyone how strong I am.

What scares you more – being trapped in space where no one can hear you scream, or an alien bursting out of your insides?
Definitely the alien in my insides. Having had a baby, it's hectic enough as it is. But if I knew something foreign was in me, moving around... I think that's why the whole Elizabeth Shaw situation – when she realized she was pregnant with the alien – would be the most terrifying thing. ●

1 / Tess Haubrich as Private Rosenthal is shocked by the discoveries the crew make on the planet

CALLIE HERNANDEZ AS
UPWORTH

We talk to **Callie Hernandez** about her character Upworth,
whose adherence to protocol puts her at odds with others...

*A*lien: Covenant Official Collector's Edition: Can you introduce us to the character you play in *Alien: Covenant*?

Callie Hernandez: Upworth is an expert in communications and is married to Ricks – who has expertise in navigation. They share those duties. She's a bit of a firecracker. She's funny. It's kind of weird because you don't really get to know the characters before chaos ensues. Ricks and Upworth are newlyweds and the youngest of the crew in terms of couplings and they really balance each other a lot.

So where Upworth thinks at a quicker pace than everybody else, she's a little bit in her own world. In that sense, the way she connects with people is through the computer system.

Ricks has a softer side than Upworth does. She's the boss and takes the reins quite a bit in terms of their relationship and the way they work together. She's a couple of steps ahead of everybody, in that she thinks before she speaks, so he's always trying to manage that with her. They balance each other out in a really beautiful way. If Upworth is a bit more headstrong, he's a bit more grounded.

As a navigator and pilot, Upworth and Tennessee also have a close connection. Tell us about that.
Tennessee really represents the love in this film. For me, the connection between Tennessee and Upworth is that he's really torn because his loved ones are somewhere he can't go, while she's trying to be the voice of reason. I think Tennessee has a heart of gold and, given the circumstances, he tends to react based on emotion. Upworth

> ## "
> ## Upworth thinks at a quicker pace than everyone else.
> ## „

becomes the voice of reason – or tries to – but she has her own issues and is grappling with them. You don't know how you're going to react until you're in the situation. Upworth is attempting to get through to Tennessee while he's in this state of insane uncertainty. So there's some push and pull in that dynamic under the circumstances.

Upworth is, essentially, sticking up for protocol. But it doesn't mean she's not equally as torn. There's a pivotal moment when she's trying to get through to Tennessee to bring him back to the situation and what is at stake. When love is in the picture, things tend to go out of the window. As much as she's fighting for protocol, there's a pivotal moment where she's trying to connect with Tennessee, and Ricks, her husband, basically says, "Stop," and she turns around. She realizes she has her husband with her, and if it were him in trouble, she can't say she wouldn't do the same thing.

What were your impressions of the set, particularly the Bridge?
I pretty much don't leave the Bridge in the film – it really does transport you to another world, and it does create a sense of claustrophobia. It's like island fever, only on this tiny ship surrounded by this giant velvet sky. You're floating in outer space in this tiny little vessel and the sets give you a sense of that. You suddenly feel very small, and the bridge itself feels small. There are hydraulics on the Bridge, so whenever we're shooting a scene and it's supposed to be shaking, we're really shaking. A couple of us would get weirdly seasick after a couple of days. It's from being in this tiny space. So the set design is just genius. ●

1/ Upworth (Callie Hernandez) in her element, at the controls of the *Covenant*'s computer system

COSTUMING
COVENANT

Janty Yates brought her many years
of experience working with Ridley
Scott to bear on costuming the
Covenant crew…

Alien: Covenant Official Collector's Edition: How did you get involved with this film?

Janty Yates: I've been very fortunate to have worked with Ridley Scott before, and we had been talking about the premise of *Alien: Covenant* even a year before we did *The Martian*. So I was kind of in the know, but not in the know.

How does *Alien* differ from other sci-fi films?

I think the first *Alien* really broke the mold in the visuals, because that spaceship was grubby; it was lived in. Their clothes were worn and there was actually a uniform created, but it was so casual as a uniform that there are Hawaiian shirts and all sorts. It really did go completely away from the *Star Treks* and the other space visuals of before.

Ridley's always said that he didn't want to use the *Star Trek* look for the costumes, because he just didn't think they would last. They're very of their time, with the asymmetric cuts and bright colors.

How does *Alien: Covenant* being more of a horror film inform your designs?

We have to have repeats of every single garment – for stunts, for action, for dummies. That's something we have to take very much into consideration, and Ridley said all the way through, apart from the sleep suits, he didn't want everyone to wear the same thing. So the security team has tactical vests, more aggressive boots and a lot more armor. They had a lot more weapons, but everybody had to have a different look. We needed to nail that and then we could get on with the repeats. So time is always of the essence. A lot of the parkas are Second World War – Lope is wearing a submersible parka from the Second World War, from Angels costume house, that we made eight repeats of. Everything that everyone wore was ad hoc.

Does the Costume department have any specialist help for things like spacesuits?

I would like to mention a company that I can't do a film without – FBFX have worked with me since 1998 when they were making armor for me on *Gladiator*. They're special effects costume makers extraordinaire – an amazing company. On *The Martian*, they made the helmets and the backpacks for the surface suit, and the helmets, yokes and backpacks on the EVAs [Extra Vehicular Activity suits] as well. They've turned their hand to everything, and where we have this enormous conundrum is how you'd make a prop mobile. I think they dread it, but they love the challenge, and they came up with this genius pivoting. We've turned into technical engineers, this costume department, but thanks to Michael Mooney and FBFX, we seem to be able to get it done.

Do you have to work closely with the Creatures or the Special Effects teams?

Costume always works closely with Creatures and Special Effects more than Visual Effects, although Visual Effects always need our costumes on the actors to completely scan them so they can use them in the future. But ▶

1/ Spacesuits in the *Covenant*'s airlock

2 / Daniels (Katherine Waterston) wears her late husband Jacob's clothes as she talks to Walter (Michael Fassbender)

3 / Daniels suited up and ready for action

2 /

DAVID/WALTER

JANTY YATES TELLS US ABOUT OUTFITTING THE TWO SYNTHETICS, DAVID AND WALTER...

Regarding David and Walter – Walter Robot 217, I think he is, is very much a scientist. He's a scientist-astronaut. We dressed him the same way as everybody else, as he is part of that team.

David, however, has been on this planet since he landed there ten years earlier, and he has had no recourse to any new clothing, because there's hardly any clothing there on the planet. He just manages to cloak himself. So he wears the spacesuit, with ten years' distress on it. The cloak he would have just found on an Engineer on the planet, and he certainly doesn't wear it for warmth. I think he just wears it so he can disguise himself when he's checking out the scientist-astronauts.

3

DANIELS

JANTY YATES ON COSTUMING KATHERINE WATERSTON AS DANIELS...

To talk about individuals' costuming is relevant for Daniels, because actually, she's bereaved at the beginning. She loses her husband early on, and she's completely devastated, but she's got to carry on. It's very endearing. She basically, after they've got up and out of the sleep suits, wears his clothes until they actually go down to the planet. When she goes down to the planet, she wears I think one of the most fabulous outfits. I love how she looks – it's grape green, with a ruched crop top and a quilted waistcoat underneath, and these great moleskin trousers with about 900 pockets on them. Katherine can wear anything – she's my clotheshorse, but she also looked great in Daniels' husband's jackets and hoodies, because she's completely devastated. She's actually more quirky than any of the others. Then she kicks some ass in the third act in the spacesuit as well, so that's pretty exciting.

► with any form of fighting, with any form of stunts, we work very hand-in-glove with Special Effects. Even for the slightest bullet wound, we need to create new costumes. With Creatures, they just need the occasional dummy, so they need a costume for that. All of that adds up in our repeat costumes tally.

You've described the film before as being in three parts. Can you talk us through that?

I describe the film as three parts from a Costume department view, because it's three acts really. In the first act, the scientist-astronauts are onboard, in hyper-sleep. They're guarding the 2,000 souls who are frozen, and they're in sleep suits. The suits were designed by Craig Green – they're wonderful, white cotton suits with ruching, and some wear balaclavas, like Formula One racing drivers. Then, something happens and they have to discuss it, and they're wearing onboard wear. Ridley loved a designer called James Long's mesh jackets. We tried to incorporate those with a more casual look.

Act two's costumes are very

much explorer wear, and we were hugely influenced by [the French artist] Moebius, who Ridley loves. We've gone back to [his influence] on a couple of films. Moebius created this character I call the Space Cowboy, and we took his atmosphere, but didn't use his exact look. We took his hat, which is based on a French Foreign Legion kepi, and every actor looks really cool in it. We did wonderful takes on outdoor wear, again designed by Craig Green with ruching, and made in Ridley's palette in waterproof fabrics. They're covered in circuitry, which monitors their bodily functions. We gave them wonderful canvas gaiters – which is a bit First World War – on their boots. They have huge backpacks, because obviously, they're going off to explore this new planet. I said, "Shouldn't they just go in spacesuits, Ridley?" and he replied, "Dude. There's oxygen there."

The last act is all spacesuits, and we've designed a loose-fitting silver spacesuit with another of FBFX's amazing helmets, this time in carbon fiber, fully lighting the actors with L.E.D. lights, 2,000

of them inside, and totally wired for sound, completely air-flowing, with GoPros working. It's a huge amount to take on board, but we've honed our craft.

What's the design process with Ridley like?

The design process is incredibly collaborative with Ridley. It's fantastic, because he's a genius – he's incredibly involved and very visual. He's from an art college background, and a production designer, and he draws all the time. So I would sit down for example with the concept artists, Dan Walker and Michael Mooney, and we would hash out some ideas on Ridley's basic brief, and then it's always prototyping, seeing exactly what Ridley thinks.

Ridley has a huge collaborative involvement in the visuals of costume, which is great. He basically will draw something that he would see, for example the greenhouse helmet, which obviously came from Moebius, but he drew it in his visuals. So we just worked to that and took the credit (*Laughs*). Not really. ●

4 / Walter (Michael Fassbender) in the Covenant crew expeditionary gear, complete with kepi-inspired hat

5 / David (Michael Fassbender) as the crew first see him, in his Engineer-salvaged cloak

6 / The 'Big Yellow' spacesuit worn by Alexander England as Ankor

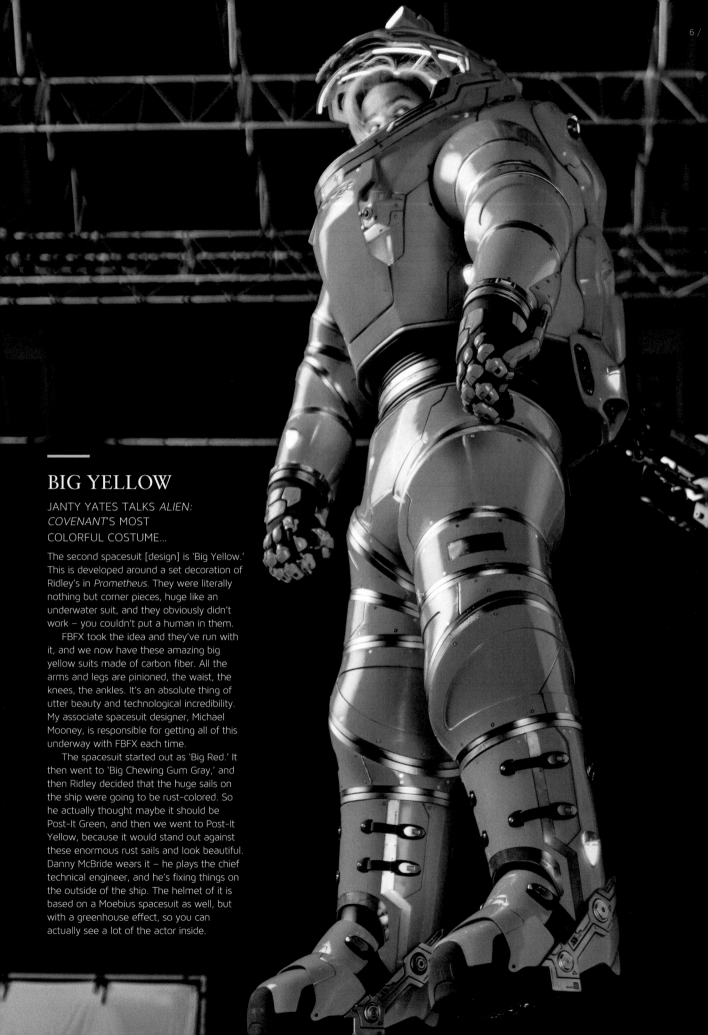

BIG YELLOW

JANTY YATES TALKS *ALIEN: COVENANT*'S MOST COLORFUL COSTUME...

The second spacesuit [design] is 'Big Yellow.' This is developed around a set decoration of Ridley's in *Prometheus*. They were literally nothing but corner pieces, huge like an underwater suit, and they obviously didn't work – you couldn't put a human in them.

FBFX took the idea and they've run with it, and we now have these amazing big yellow suits made of carbon fiber. All the arms and legs are pinioned, the waist, the knees, the ankles. It's an absolute thing of utter beauty and technological incredibility. My associate spacesuit designer, Michael Mooney, is responsible for getting all of this underway with FBFX each time.

The spacesuit started out as 'Big Red.' It then went to 'Big Chewing Gum Gray,' and then Ridley decided that the huge sails on the ship were going to be rust-colored. So he actually thought maybe it should be Post-It Green, and then we went to Post-It Yellow, because it would stand out against these enormous rust sails and look beautiful. Danny McBride wears it – he plays the chief technical engineer, and he's fixing things on the outside of the ship. The helmet of it is based on a Moebius spacesuit as well, but with a greenhouse effect, so you can actually see a lot of the actor inside.

CONCEPT ART - THE HALL OF HEADS
The crew discover the Engineers'
astounding Hall of Heads...

ALIEN VISIONS

Alien: Covenant takes us into new worlds, and it's Cinematographer **Dariusz Wolski** who helps bring those images to the screen...

*A*lien: Covenant Official Collector's Edition: What do you think makes the *Alien* films so special?

Dariusz Wolski: I saw the first *Alien* when I'd just arrived in the States from Poland – I'd graduated from Polish film school then. At that age you're extremely susceptive to visuals because you just want to be a cameraman, and *Alien* was a film that left a tremendous impression on me.

The first unique thing about it was that it's a movie set in the future and at that time, the future was usually portrayed in a *Star Trek* or *Star Wars* way, where everything was very clean, pristine and glossy. And here you are in this very claustrophobic environment that is a spaceship, but it's gritty, and water's dripping. That was the first thing that struck me – that's a future that was way more interesting than whatever I'd seen so far. So Ridley Scott is basically responsible for setting up the completely new vision of what the future would look like, contrary to whatever we'd seen in *Star Wars*, *Star Trek* and even, as a matter of fact, Kubrick's *2001*. That's the first thing that struck me. And also the way he dramatically showed – or maybe didn't show – the Alien. The scariest part of it is how little you see, and that's what makes your imagination [run wild] and that's the smartest trick I've ever known. Now, with all the technology, we show everything and quite often people miss the point. ▶

What sets this film apart from *Prometheus*?

It's more of an adventure – I would say it's more horror-driven. It's more scary, more in your face. It's very gruesome – it's definitely R-rated, but with a lot of class. That's what *Alien* was – *Alien* was a movie that was a classic horror film, yet done by an artist.

[*Prometheus*] was much cleaner, and it's kind of an homage to *2001*. It's a lot more philosophical in a way. Now, with *Alien: Covenant*, Ridley's going back to his roots. When we talked about doing this film, we really wanted to go back to a very pure horror, rough, gritty look, which I think we've accomplished.

Ridley established a very distinct look on the first film 30 years ago. How much does that influence the choices you're making on this movie?

Very strongly. The original *Alien* influenced me, and this film is strongly influenced by the original *Alien*. It's trying to be a modern version of that, using modern technology, because technology's way different now, so you can go further than they did, not having the limitations of 1978. A lot of the conversation with Ridley has been about how this stuff was done, how we are doing it now, and how the whole thing has evolved.

It's quite amazing, because it's just very simple lighting fixtures on the ship that are just super-thin LEDs controlled by dimmers. Back then, there had to be a light and tracing paper and a fixture on top of it. Everything was melting and was super-hot and there was never enough light. I'd say we have it easy now.

During the course of the film, we see three key environments: the *Covenant*, the planet and inside the Engineers' structures. Could you explain your approach to each of these environments?

On the spaceship, the approach is

2 /

to make it look as interesting as possible with modern technology. We're basically lighting it with lighting fixtures that are actually in the ship, so you use very little complementary lighting, if any. We used a lot of LED lights, but we covered them in different fixtures because we're trying to get away from the fluorescent-tube look that's been done for so many years. We put the strips of LED lights in different tubes with varying patterns on them just to make them different.

The whole approach to *Covenant*, unlike *Prometheus*, is that this ship is way more utilitarian. It's not very high-tech, so the lights are harsher, and that goes back to our original idea about making this movie look rougher.

For the planet we took inspiration from the actual weather in Milford Sound – it's very cloudy, with a soft light. There are mountains that appear and disappear in the clouds, and everything is drizzling. That's the thing we've taken from the original environment, and that we tried to repeat on the back lot. We insisted on having everything really gray and fogged and soft. It's like constant dawn or dusk.

When we go inside [to the Dreadnought], we wanted to have

a very 18th-Century, painterly look – the light comes from the source, which from those paintings has to come from candles. So we invented lights which were motion-controlled. When we want to play the scene, the light is on. We wanted the lighting to be more organic, so I ended up having sources of light and then we would take them out, shoot the plates, and the VFX people would create this constantly floating lava lamp source that was motion-activated. There are only a few scenes like that, but I think they're very powerful. So it's complete darkness, they come in, the light comes on, and when they go away, it goes away.

It's especially important in the scenes where David meets his 'brother,' Walter, and in particular, when David is teaching Walter how to play the flute. We designed the motion-control shot so he could play two characters as one continuous shot. There are no tricks with cutting or anything. It was purely one take, which is amazing when you see it cut.

Tell us about shooting the Lander descent.

They have to go through this barrier [that surrounds the planet], so Neil Corbould, a great effects guy from England, put the Lander ▶

1 / Previous spread: A discovery aboard the Engineers' Dreadnought 2 / The *Covenant* crew explores the forbidding-looking Dreadnought 3 / A Xenomorph appears, complete with water effects

4/

6/

5 /

▶ on a powerful shaker. Sometimes
when you do those scenes, you
just shake the camera. But it's
not about shaking the camera;
it's about what happens to a face
when you shake it, and that's
when you get a real effect. You
actually try not to shake the
camera, but everything is shaking
and you can see the actors reacting
to it, because they can't sit still.
So that was very powerful, and
complemented with lights and
light from outside. We shot a
lot of plates using a helicopter
in New Zealand, going through
rain, fog and clouds, and
revealing landscape. There's a
whole sequence from being in
space to shaking, as there's a
storm out there.

The landing was shot in
Milford Sound, this beautiful
fjord in New Zealand, and we
built the ship partially, because
we needed the characters to
get out of it. The landing of
course will be CG. In our real
environment, we always do
effects, so we had speedboats and
helicopters churning the water.
We used this combination of
five cameras on one lake, so the
image is huge – you can pan and
scan, and it's really impressive.

**How did you decide to shoot the
Neomorph birth in Medbay?**
We decided to play the scene

really bright. The cliché is that
if something is scary, then it's dark
and you don't see it, and that
comedy has to be bright and funny.

So when Ledward gets infected
and eventually gives birth to the
baby alien, we made it really
bright, because it's an operating
table. It's super-bright – so bright
that it's scary. That was our
aesthetic decision.

**How about the attack in the
long grass?**
We shot most of it in New

Zealand, and dramatically
[speaking], Faris has tried to shoot
the alien and blows up the whole
ship. Then right after that, there's
this scene in the grass. It's in
the proximity of the ship that's
burning, so my approach was to
light the whole thing with the
flames coming off the ship.

We had a partial ship – it
will be finished digitally – and
along with a lot of strong lights
far away, the whole thing is lit
by the flames. So, it's like this
orange, flickering light. Some of

4 / A single flashlight illuminates a Face-Hugger's surprise attack 5 / Breaking with tradition, the carnage of the Neomorph
birth is captured in a brightly-lit, white environment

7 /

8 /

it is silhouetted, some is front-lit, some was on grass and we shot quite a bit there. We had a problem, though, because the location we'd chosen was tide-dependent, so we had to schedule everything to come in at low tide. Then the place in the grass was elevated so that when the water came in, we could still shoot. By the end, we had a ship in the distance, half-submerged in water. It was quite beautiful.

Were there any challenges in David's lab?
That was the environment I was describing earlier, where it's triggered by those lava lights. You make a decision if you have a long dialogue scene in one place, so we had those lights coming on and off. Here, there's action going on, so you just limit that. You don't want to draw too much attention, so there's one light and everything else is very sporadic. But it's still [lit] within the environment – with those lava lamps. It comes right before the egg room, which is

really dark. The flashlights come on there, and it's really dark and you don't see anything until it's lit by flashlight. The death of Oram is in the egg room and that's literally lit by one flashlight, because he got knocked out, so he dropped it. So the flashlight is conveniently aiming at his gut when the alien comes out. [*Laughs*]

How about the David vs. Walter fight?
That's in the Hall of Heads. Again it's the Engineers' environment planet, and it's this huge room with seven of [these heads]. So this fight scene starts in the scrolls room, and then on the big stairs leading to the Hall of Heads and that was lit with what we call no-light moonlight, just to be able to read the faces there. We had some fire, because when they get to the Hall of Heads, that's where they camp, so they start the fires to stay warm. So those fires are still there. The whole world of the Engineers is futuristic but ancient – it's stone, it's fire, it's water, yet it's high-tech.

What was your biggest challenge on this film?
I'd say weather always is, because there's nothing you can do about it. You wake up every morning and just pray. We got so fortunate in New Zealand, because the chances of having this cloudy weather is pretty high there.

We had this forest set in Potts Hill, an area of gigantic trees that are replicas of Sequoia trees, so we built trunks up to 25 feet up and then the challenge is – what's on top? There's no canopy. So we built this really elaborate canopy system on wires with big square shadows. It was all great, and perfectly engineered, but when we showed up, the wind came up and there was nothing you could do. Day One, we had to just work around it, and Day Two, it worked. But you're just building something so huge like you build a ship. It hits the storm, and it's going to crash no matter how much it cost. But I've loved doing a lot of movies in different environments. ●

7 / The stunning scenery of Milford Sound provides a counterpoint to Karine and Ledward's fear and pain 8 / A Xenomorph makes its presence known...

THE XENOMORPH

The original creature from Ridley Scott's *Alien* in 1979, the Xenomorph has rightly become an iconic creature in the realms of sci-fi horror. The *Alien: Covenant Official Collector's Edition* takes a closer look at the alien monster of our nightmares…

The Xenomorph, once it has burst from the chest of its host's body, grows incredibly rapidly, eventually becoming larger than a human and far stronger. Xenomorphs are fast and deadly, striking at their prey with both their inner and outer jaws, as well as their spiked tails.

Xenomorphs are incredibly difficult to kill, as their blood is a highly corrosive acid. Trying to kill a Xenomorph can therefore result in injury to yourself and others, as well as damage to your surroundings. This acid can even burn through metal, such as the bulkheads of a ship.

Xenomorphs are surprisingly intelligent and fiendishly cunning, and are therefore not to be underestimated. The Xenomorph will always find a way to get to you, no matter where you are!

1 / A creature design image shows the Xenomorph's sinewy, almost skeletal form

2 / A close-up of a model of the Xenomorph reveals its outer jaws, ready to open and reveal its inner jaws

1 /

3 /

4 /

5 /

THE FACE-HUGGER

Hatched from an egg, the Face-Hugger launches itself at the face of its host, gripping on by means of its eight powerful legs and strong prehensile tail.

Like the Xenomorph itself, the Face-Hugger has corrosive acid for blood, making it practically impossible to remove. Once it latches on, its host is powerless to stop the Face-Hugger depositing its parasitoid larvae in the pharynx, impregnating them.

The Xenomorph offspring eventually exits the host by bursting violently through their chest, inevitably killing the host in the process.

6/

3 / The iconic profile of the Xenomorph shows its elongated cranium and dorsal spikes

4 / The detail of the Xenomorph's inner and outer jaws is seen as a special effects artist works on a model of the Xenomorph for *Alien: Covenant*

5 / A dissected Face-Hugger egg in David's Lab shows the Face-Hugger coiled and ready to launch out

6 / Oram (Billy Crudup) struggles against a Face-Hugger's attack

7 / A model shot of the Xenomorph shows the detailing of its head, ribcage and spine

7/

OTHER GREAT TIE-IN COMPANIONS FROM TITAN

ON SALE NOW!

Star Trek: The Movies
ISBN 9781785855924

Fifty Years of Star Trek
ISBN 9781785855931

Star Trek - A Next Generation Companion
ISBN 9781785855948

Rogue One - The Official Collector's Edition
ISBN 9781785861574

Rogue One - The Official Mission Debrief
ISBN 9781785861581

The Best of Star Wars Insider Volume 1
ISBN 9781785851162

The Best of Star Wars Insider Volume 2
ISBN 9781785851179

The Best of Star Wars Insider Volume 3
ISBN 9781785851896

The Best of Star Wars Insider Volume 4
ISBN 9781785851902

Star Wars: Lords of the Sith
ISBN 9781785851919

AVAILABLE FROM TITAN BOOKS

Alien: Covenant - The Official Movie Novelization
9781785654787

The Art and Making of Alien: Covenant
9781785653810

Alien - The Archive
9781783291045

TITANCOMICS TITANBOOKS

For more information visit www.titan-comics.com and www.titan-books